Divination Through the Ages

Divination Through the Ages

By Reverend Ellen Wallace Douglas

Also by author:
The Laughing Christ
El's Rae: A Memoir
Homeward Bound
Be Still and Know
The Peaceful Silence
Concordance of The Aquarian Gospel of Jesus the Christ
Home to the Light
The Beckoning Light

Order this book online at www.trafford.com
or email orders@trafford.com

Most Trafford titles are also available at major online book retailers.

Printed in the United States of America.

ISBN: 978-1-4669-5354-3 (sc)
ISBN: 978-1-4669-5355-0 (e)

Trafford rev. 08/21/2012

 www.trafford.com

North America & international
toll-free: 1 888 232 4444 (USA & Canada)
phone: 250 383 6864 ♦ fax: 812 355 4082

To all the psychics and mediums through history who have, with honesty and integrity, provided others with comfort and guidance from entities in the spirit world of God.

"You will never know the world aright till the Sea floweth in your Veins, till you are Clothed with the Heavens, and Crowned with the Stars; And perceive yourself to be the Sole Heir of the Whole World; And more then so, because Men are in it who are every one Sole Heirs, as well as you. Till you are intimately Acquainted with that Shady Nothing out of which this World was made; Till your spirit filleth the whole World and the Stars are your Jewels; Till you love men so as to Desire their Happiness with a thirst equal to the zeal of your own."

-- Thomas Traherne

Contents

Preface

In the context of this book, divination will refer to any kind of prophecy, necromancy, prognostication, psychism, mediumship, or any other method used to open a channel of communication to the spirit world or to determine the future of a leader, individual, or group by contacting the spirit world of God.

This book exists because I believe there is a need for it. I have been collecting books about spirit communication for several decades. I have found only one that explains some of the history of divination. Manas, in his Divination, Ancient and Modern, provides details of the sibyls and oracles of ancient times. He also notes modern aspects of divination. Several other books describe some kinds of divination and their expression. Now I would like to combine a history showing the continuity of divination through the ages, the various kinds of divination found in the Bible and explain some of the kinds (there is a plethora of them) of divination.

Divination is fundamentally communication between earthlings and the spirit world. I was raised in the Universalist Church and was married in a Presbyterian church. The first forty plus years of my life I never heard of communication with the 'dead'. I put 'dead' in quotes because now I know there is no death. Of course we all should know it, since Jesus the Christ demonstrated it two thousand years ago.

My first encounter with a professional medium was when I was forty-nine. I was employed in the north country of New York State. Only one other employee shared the office with me. One day she told me she had become a 'believer' after receiving a message from a local medium, and urged me to go see her, in the village of Lake George. After making an appointment for a reading, I met Millie Coutant. The first thing she saw was a tall, good-looking man standing behind me. He was my father, who had passed when I was five. He said, "I couldn't catch my breath", and I suddenly realized he was explaining to me how he died forty-five years earlier! He had a heart attack at fifty-eight, with no history of illness of any kind.

Then he said, through Millie, "I am waiting for you. I want to show you around. The light is different here; the colors are different." In that first reading Millie also 'saw' a scar from a female operation, and told me that the dreams I had about water were to help me be calm, as my workplace was very noisy. She closed with the comment, "I see you as a teacher, ringing a bell to call in the children." I told her I was not a teacher, and she responded that it was a past life she saw.

Afterward, as I recalled the amazing content and source of the messages, I wondered if she could tell me about more of my past lives. I called her for the second appointment and asked if she could describe them. She told me that she could not guarantee that, but she would try. See text of manuscript for my past lives described by Millie.

Archangel Gabriel visited the Earth for twelve years (1987-1999), channeling through a dedicated Christian Metaphysical Bishop. Also, in 1995 Jesus the Christ came for the first time, through the same devoted channel. He alternated with Gabriel in teaching us, from 1995 to 1999. On two occasions Jesus came to teach us in the morning, and Gabriel came in the afternoon. Gabriel explained what an extraordinary feat for Rev. Penny this was, because the energy of an archangel – who never existed on the earth plane – is vastly different from the energy of one who has lived on the earth plane many times (Jesus). An archangel's energy is of an extremely high vibration. A few seminars were presented by Jesus only. All their teachings are available in print or recordings. See Bibliography.

Gabriel said that eleven master teachers also came at the same time, to various places on Earth, to teach the same lesson that he brought: Every human being is a child of God. All humanity is the 'only begotten Son of God'. God created us from Himself. God is love, therefore so are we. Gabriel also explained how all our experiences are created by us, therefore we have the power to uncreate them. He told us that we are ready for his lessons, or he would not bother to come.

Gabriel taught us so much about the angel world; the spirit world of God. In *Angels, Earthlings and Aliens* (7/27/91), he described all the archangels, including himself. He is the Announcer of the Ages. He came 2,000 years ago and announced to Mary that she would birth Jesus the Christ. He announced to Elizabeth that she would birth John, who became the Baptist. That was the beginning of the Age of Pisces. This is the beginning of the Age of Aquarius, or, as Gabriel called it, the Age of Truth; the Age of Spirituality. He told us that Rev. Penny Donovan (channeler of himself and Jesus the Christ) had been learning for 500 years of earth time to prepare herself for the task. He described the spirit world as a place of light and love, peace and joy. He told us of the entities who reside there, describing in detail their functions. This is a very brief overview:

Archangels – six beside himself.
Angels – layer upon layer of angelic beings who do the will of God, as directed.
Ascended Masters – who have lived upon the Earth, then ascended and now come to assist earthlings on our spiritual path.

Teachers – come to Earth to help us learn about life and ourselves.

Guides – who help direct our spiritual path.

Devas and sprites – spirit entities who come to assist animals and plants on their path.

All these entities have the ability to communicate with us. And we have the ability to communicate with them. All we need to do is accept our capacity to do so, and use it.

Anyone who is unwilling to accept the idea of communication with the spirit world of God is denying himself the broader vistas of the world God created. The good news is that eventually everyone will.

All of these experiences of mine led me to the decision to write this book. Part I explains the history of divination, and the existence of communication between humans and other forms of life. Now is the time to wake up to these avenues of communication so that all might learn and grow and become aware of the more that we already are.

Part II describes the various kinds of divination.

Quotations from the Bible are printed in italics, to show the author's reverence for the words in that sacred book.

Grateful acknowledgment is given to Maria, who transferred this book to the publisher in an efficient and meticulous manner.

Joyful acknowledgment also to my friends Marylou Krywe and Grace Abbott, who willingly and patiently assisted me in editing and proofreading.

Appreciative acknowledgment to Karen Lafler for front and back cover art.

Introduction

This book is based on the assumption that all things on Earth emanate from on high; from a world of spirit which is eternal. This assumption comes from the ancient adage 'as above, so below'.

Divination, From the *Encyclopedia of Religion*: "Practices aiming at gaining knowledge of future or otherwise unknown events. In the O. T., diviners are listed among influential men, together with judges, prophets and elders". (Is. iii, 2).[1]

Mr. Manas, in his book *Divination Ancient and Modern* says this: "Divination is an art, and, as such, it has to be mastered through patient effort and spiritual illumination. Certain brain, etheric and mental centers have to be opened and certain dormant faculties developed."[2]

Many forms of divination have been described in the world, from ancient cave life to recent years. For example, "Astrology is older than history. There is some evidence that Cro-Magnon man may have followed the cycles of the stars, notching bones to aid his substandard memory in creating an almanac."[3]

The premise of all psychism is the belief that there is a method of communication available between humans and the next world, the spirit world of God. There are many names for this communication, among which are: ESP – extra-sensory perception, mental telepathy; 'mind reading', the sixth sense [beyond the five senses of the body], and the third eye -- between the eyebrows, also known as the sixth chakra.

" . . . not withstanding skepticism and ridicule, prophecy is a phenomenon that for thousands of years has sunk deep roots into the consciousness of humanity, and fails to be eradicated . . . the belief in prophecy cannot wholly die out anymore than the belief in goodness, or spirituality, or culture."[4]

This historical belief opened the door long ago to the possibility of prophecy. Now it is time to acknowledge the *probability* of it.

The universality of interest in prophecy

"Scholars in several fields – biblical studies, history of religions, anthropology, and sociology – study prophets, but they tend to have different interests and to study different individuals."[5]

Ancient beginnings of prophecy: "Prophecy, which Plato called 'the noblest of the arts,' was experienced by the ancient world chiefly through oracles."[6]

Many people publicly deny their belief in divination of one kind or another, yet privately they seek a medium/psychic to know about the future. And newspapers would not print a daily horoscope unless there was interest in reading it. "Today we laugh at prophecies, though many of us at least secretly believe in them." [7]

In 1940, Mr. H.J. Forman wrote: "Not only were critical times in the past the objects of often strikingly correct prophesying before the event, but even our own crucial period, through which we are now passing, has long been foretold, with considerable detail, by a very chorus of voices crying in the wilderness. Our immediate present and future, it would appear, have been the concern of ages of seers, and if events have taken us unawares, it is owing largely, as any student of prophecy can demonstrate, to our own perversity and blindness." Stor of Prophecy. [8]

We base all our decisions on the past, even though the path behind us is strewn with guilt, anger, destruction, and wars. "If past lives, parallel – lives and a sixth (psychic) sense are in fact reality, then there is a reason for these realities. There is a universal law and it is certainly time to understand it, for we are here on earth living our lives for a *purpose*. Until we can comprehend that purpose and the full extent of our powers and abilities, we make our lives more difficult than they need to be." [9]

Prophecy has always existed. We live in a world of illusion, according to *A Course in Miracles,* when the real world is the world unseen. It is not populated by 'dead' people but the living people we once knew on Earth. It is that spirit world which is the world of God, angels and our guides and teachers. They long to communicate with us, but we must open our minds and hearts to the idea, and then learn from them how to live a positive, fulfilling life while here.

Oracles and seers
"The Oracles and seers of ancient Greece practiced divination . . . their (oracles) prophecies were understood to be the will of the gods verbatim. Because of the high demand for oracle consultations and the oracles' limited work schedule, they were not the main source of divination for the ancient Greeks. That role fell to the seers (*mateis* in Greek). . . [10]

Oracles were for rulers; seers, who received information from creatures and signs. "Seers were not in direct contact with the gods; instead, they were interpreters of signs provided by the gods. Seers used many methods to explicate the will of the gods including . . . bird signs, etc. They were more numerous than the oracles and did not keep a limited schedule; thus, they were highly valued by all Greeks, not just those with the capacity to travel to Delphi or other such distant sites."[11]

COSMIC LAWS
There are cosmic laws upon which prophecy is founded. The cosmic plane and cosmic laws are the same now as in times of early humankind. What happens today in the field of psychic phenomena happened with the Sibyls and Oracles of the ancient past. Knowledge unattainable by the finite mind was made available by Apollo (then) and now by various spirit entities, through a natural or trained medium or psychic.

In the 17th century Emanuel Swedenborg experienced communication with many in the spirit world, over a period of several years. This scientific genius then wrote volumes about the lessons he had learned from the higher realms. Although a scientific genius, he has not been recognized generally because of his belief in spirit communication and a huge number of experiences which he tells of in his visits to the spirit world.

"As the law of vibration rules supreme on all planes . . . only a pure and unselfish diviner will send out high spiritual vibrations, which in turn will attract and make possible his communication with a correspondingly high discarnate entity, or the pattern of higher thoughts from the spiritual realm of the Cosmos."[12]

To be more explicit, the psychic person is able to read the akashic records, which bear record of the actions and thoughts of every human throughout all time. *The Akashic Records* is an invisible dimension, a Hall of Records, where *all* thoughts and experiences are stored. All information there can be contacted psychically."[13]

PROPHECY AND PSYCHIC OCCURENCES
Throughout recorded time, from the ancient world to the present people have sought to see and understand supernatural events and experiences. ". . . 'supernatural' occurrences have been reported in all countries, and in all ages of the world's history. In Egypt, Chaldea, Babylon, Persia, India, China, Greece, and Rome, we find the same manifestations recorded as we encounter today in the drawing-rooms of New York, London, and Paris! [14]

The history of spirit communication and psychic phenomena has been a fascinating journey, beginning with serious guidance (from sibyls and oracles) to prohibition against prophecy, to scientific investigation of today.

". . . From Balaam to Bacon, and from Mother Shipton to Madame de Thebes, have prophesied, and only a very voluminous work could take note of all recorded prophecies. . . . Today, quite serious students are giving scientific attention to psychical research, telepathy and clairvoyance, and people like William James, Madame Curie, Lord Rayleigh, Sir Oliver Lodge, Dr. Osty of Paris, and Dr. Alexis Carrel have not disdained to make their interest known."[15]

To ridicule and disbelieve what we learn from spirit communication is to throw the baby out with the bathwater: "It is conceivable, of course, observes an English scholar, that all virtue is a sham, and that all predictions are a fiction, but the balance of probability is the other way.

The false prophecies do not discredit the true any more than the spuriousness of the letters of Plato discredits the authenticity of the dialogues of Plato." [16]

Of course there are false prophets, as well as true prophets. Did not God give us the ability to discern one from the other? In the Bible we find: *Beloved, Believe not every spirit, but try the spirits whether they are of God: because many false prophets are gone out into the world.* I John 4:1

Do we not have an innate sense of the 'good' and 'bad'? Also, who benefits from prophecy?

" . . prophecy very seldom profited the prophet and on numerous occasions it led to his martyrdom and death.
"Roughly and briefly, prophecy may be defined as clairvoyance in space and time." [17]

"Today we no longer so readily think of uncomprehended phenomena as supernatural – but more simply as nature thus far unexplained." [18]

Heaven's sacred aspects, as provided by a woman awaking from a three year coma:

> "There is a depth, a mystery to all that pertains to the divine life, which I dare not try to describe; I could not if I would, I would not if I could. A sacredness enfolds it all that curious eyes should not look upon. Suffice it to say, that no joy we know on earth, however rare, however sacred, can be more than the faintest shadow of the joy we there find; no dreams of rapture, here unrealized, approach the bliss of one moment, even, in that divine world. No sorrow; no pain; no sickness; no death; no partings; no disappointments; no tears but those of joy; no broken hopes; no mislaid plans; no night, nor storm, nor shadows even; but light and joy and love and peace and rest forever and forever. 'Amen,' and again my heart says reverently, 'Amen'." [19]

Heaven is the spirit world of God. Heaven, or 'the other side' is where we all go upon so-called 'death'. There is no death, as so clearly demonstrated by the Master Jesus 2,000 years ago. It is here on Earth that we are strangers. This is the 'far country' to which the prodigal son, as well as all of us humans, has traveled. "Your chosen home is on the other side, beyond the veil." [20]

John Keats addressed the idea of two worlds: "Can death be sleep, when life is but a dream?"

Originally, science included such beliefs as astrology and revelation. Later revelation was relegated to certain 'religious' individuals, and astrology became astronomy – an exact science. Astrology then got a 'bad name', as though one's birth date no longer had any significance as to the sign it was born under, or its relation to the planets.

SCIENCE AND DIVINATION
"Essentially, science was learned through divine "revelation", although it was also the object of experimental observation. Scientific study was the privilege of a caste, the scribes and priests, and it was handed down carefully by strict traditional methods in the circles of the "initiated". . . The heavens, the world of the divinities, were painstakingly scrutinized. Periodic celestial phenomena, such as eclipses, were known and could be foretold. Still, the true Mesopotamian 'sciences' were divination and magic."[21]

When scripture refers to 'church' it is not making note of a building as we know it, but rather a place of worship in the wilderness that mostly existed at that time. Cities and towns were far apart and embedded in forests and plains. As the years unfolded erecting structures for all purposes, including worship, became a common thing.

Worship and divination
"Place of worship were built everywhere . . . Particularly notable was the great pointed tower, magnificently decorated, which was called a 'ziggurat.' This impressive monument, which seems to have been regarded as a place for meeting with the divinity when it came to visit its people in this world below, was admirably suited to the splendors of the official liturgy." [22]

xviii

This makes clear reference to the fact that there is a spirit world which is inhabited by entities related to people on Earth and who *visit the world below*. We are reminded of John 4:24: *God is a spirit: and they that worship him must worship him in spirit and in truth*.

Articles used in divination – from animal entrails and cloud formations to tarot cards and tea leaves – it is important to remember that there is no power in those articles; they simply are a method used by mediums to invite spirit communication.

Emanuel Swedenborg, genius before his time and frequent visitor to the Astral Plane, said:
"I saw also in a vision how some beautiful bread was presented to me on a plate. This was a prediction that the Lord Himself will instruct me, as soon as I have attained that state in which all my preconceived notions will be removed from me; which is the first state of learning; or in other words that I must first become a child, and that then I shall be able to be nurtured in knowledge, as is being done with me now." [23]

This story reminded me of my own psychic experience when, in March of 1984, at my first séance. The Master Jesus came to me, manifesting in a white robe, with long auburn hair and piercing, loving, blue eyes. His arms were outstretched, palms up. In his hands laid a huge loaf of bread. He said, "Lay down your life for me and I will give you the bread of life." And he was gone.

I was unaware of it at that time, but it influenced my later decision to address the alcohol addiction which had plagued my life, and the decision led to long-term sobriety. It also convinced me, beyond any doubt, that there is a spirit world of God, inhabited by Jesus and all those who pass into spirit. And we can 'be in touch' with them at will – their will, not ours – for *ever* do we have free choice. Finally, I was convinced that we can have spirit guidance at any time we seek it.

Twenty years later, in 2004, Jesus came to me, this time through the same channel who had brought Archangel Gabriel and Jesus, and told me what my third book would be (I had already written *The Laughing Christ* and *El's Rae: A Memoir*). He said my third book would be a book of meditations based on Scripture, The Course (*A Course in Miracles*) and my own experiences. I felt somehow that I would write a third book, but I did not have a clue as to what it would be. Now, with explicit directions from Jesus, I had the content, the format, and the source! This guidance led me not only to the third book, but all the writing I did pursuant to it.

The contents of this book are permeated with words from the lessons which Archangel brought to a small group in Albany, NY from 1987 to 1999. He is the Announcer of the Ages, and this is the onset of the Age of Aquarius, also called by Gabriel the truth age. He and eleven ascended masters came to Earth, at various places, to awaken us to our true Selves, as children of God. From 1995 to 1999 Jesus also channeled messages to us, expounding on his teachings of 2,000 years ago. See Bibliography to order these messages.

Divination Through the Ages

PART ONE
HISTORY OF DIVINATION

CHAPTER 1
ANCIENT TIMES

Ancient societies have left signs that they had a belief in various kinds of prophecy and prognostication. Through all recorded time information has been found to support this constant belief system. Yet today any form of psychic talent is usually accepted only in small, private circles of friends who have a strong belief in such things. With this historical persistence it seems that we must, at some point in time, openly and publicly announce our belief in the possibility that there is another source of information available to humankind. Is it from only a few gifted people or does *all* humanity have access to it?
And what is its source if it transcends our five physical senses?

From where could this guidance come? We find in Scripture the phrase
   May be able to comprehend with all saints what is the breadth, and length, and depth, and height;
   And to know the love of Christ, which passeth knowledge, that ye might be filled with all the fullness of God. (Eph 3:18-19)

Four dimensions are noted here, and yet we live in a three-dimensional world. Obviously, there is another dimension which we have not as yet understood or defined. If that dimension enables us to know the love of Christ and allows us to be filled with the fullness of God (which is Love, *I John 4:8*), then it must be holy. And what could be more holy than the kingdom of God, which is spirit? (*God is a spirit, John 4:24*)

This 'love of Christ' is beyond human knowledge and yet is accessible to humans. There does not appear to be any place in scripture where knowledge is inaccessible to all humans. As a matter of fact, St. Luke notes:
   For there is nothing covered that shall not be revealed; neither hid, that shall not be known. (Luke 12:2).

1

His words indicate that at some future time all shall be made known to humankind. We might now ask, "Is this the accepted time?" Gabriel told us it takes 2,000 years for humanity to accept a new idea. The new idea which Jesus brought to Earth was the message he taught *and lived*: Love thy neighbor as thyself, and forgive always.

Have we really learned these new ideas? The key to acceptance of new knowledge is merely our willingness to open our minds to it. When we open our minds to the possibility of communication with the spirit world – the world of God, we shall join a hidden army of those who have accepted communication with the spirit world of God for years, privately.

Prophets of all times have been sought out and believed.

"For at least 25,000 years, shamans have played their part as . . . priests, magicians, and healers. Portraits of entranced shamans decorate the walls of Stone Age caves; even today, in parts of Asia, the Arctic and the Americas, these supposed magicians practice their arts." [1]

Besides the scrawled images on cave walls, various tools were used in ancient divination. Among items used were prayer beads (by Tibetan Buddhist lamas), yarrow stalks and dominoes (China), playing cards (gypsies), tarot cards (Egypt). Later, it was believed that the sibyls and oracles received messages directly from the gods, which made the messages credible and true. Today we use the phrase 'divinely inspired' or 'divine intervention'.

The first seers and prophets of recorded history

Even before the oracles there was a line of prophetesses, called sibyls. Of the ten major sibyls, five can be found today on the ceiling of the Sistine Chapel in the Vatican. This indicates the value which early popes placed on the prophecies of the sibyls. Another indicator is the fact that what the sibyls said was recorded for future reference.

Sibyls

Def: "Any of several prophetesses usu. accepted at 10 in number and credited to widely separate parts of the ancient world (as Babylonia, Egypt, Greece, and Italy)". [2]

Some of the sibyls recorded their words, and the writings came to be known as the Sibylline Oracles. The sibyls spoke while in trance, so it is likely that a scribe took down their words. Perhaps the scribe was the same person (the priest) who interpreted the words.

Sibylline Oracles
"Oracles or prophecies issuing from a sibyl, a woman who, in ancient times, acted at various places as a medium or mouthpiece of some god; a collection or collections of prophecies, advice, information, attributed to a sibyl or sibyls. In the days of the old Roman republic, Sibylline Books were often consulted by the magistrates for guidance in state affairs." [3]

The impact which the Sibylline Oracles had on the ancient rulers is confirmed by the fact that not years but centuries later they were still highly regarded.

Centuries later (in early Roman times) the Sibylline Oracles were still regarded as of great significance:

> "We know that before the erection of temples for the worship of God, or the gods or of the invisible forces of Nature . . . man was worshipping God privately . . . or with all other persons bound together by the same necessity, or by the same danger . . . In the same natural and logical way of evolution we can reason and say with certainty that . . . there should exist individual . . . seers and prophets, to lead the people along this line of divination and give the people guidance and advice for their material and spiritual progress and development . . . These first seers and prophets of recorded human history were the Sibyls." [4]

The five major sibyls that we find on the Sistine Chapel ceiling are:

1. Persian Sibyl
2. Libyan Sibyl
3. Delphic Sibyl
4. Cumaean Sibyl
5. Erythraean Sibyl

A brief description of each:

3

1. The Persian sibyl was a native of Persia and also known as the
Chaldean and Babylonian Sibyl or soothsayer. Those who spoke of her
were "St. Augustine, Firmianus Lactantius, the Christian writer and the
tutor of Crispus, the son of Constantine the Great . . . more than all
other Sibyls treated largely of the advent of the crucifixion of Christ
our Lord, for which she wrote eighty-four books of prophecies and
notable events as she lived a long time". [5]

She wrote, "When the time predicted shall come in which the
Redeemer is to come into the world, the sound of a voice will be heard
in the deserts, and that voice will invite all mortals to prepare the way
and cleanse their souls of vices and sins, and they will be baptized in
pure and limpid waters. . . . of the preaching and baptism of John the
Baptist, of the miracle of the five loaves and the two fishes with which
our Lord fed the five thousand people in the desert." [6]

2. The Libyan sibyl lived in Libya and is also known by Bybissa or
Elisa. "Some of her verses are quoted by Sixtus of Siena, 'which treat
upon the miracles that our Lord performed. That He was to heal the
sick and the crippled who should have faith and confidence in Him.
That the blind should have their sight restored, the lame walk, the deaf
hear, the dumb speak, the devils be driven out, and the dead rise.' She
also said that 'God was just towards all men, and was no respecter of
persons, a Holy, Living, Eternal, Everlasting King . . .' " [7]

3. The Delphic Sibyl
"This Sibyl received her name from the town of Delphi where she
lived and gave her message of Apollo, the god of light, long before the
establishment of the Delphic Oracle. . . . she was born . . . before the
Trojan War . . . she foretold in her oracles that Helen would be
brought up in Sparta to be the cause of the ruin of Asia and of Europe
and that for her sake the Greeks would capture Troy." [8]

4. The Cumaean Sibyl. "This Sibyl was a native of Cumae . . . a very
ancient Greek town on the North coast of the bay of Naples, founded
about 1050 B.C. Early historians and Christian writers mentioned her,
including Thucydides, Strabo, and Eusebiuis. "Everyone is acquainted
with the splendid narrative of Virgil regarding this Sibyl." [9]

Not all sibyls were female. The following quote reveals one sibyl as being male:

5. The Erythraean Sibyl.
> "St. Augustine is probably to be regarded as the most especial defender of the Sibylline books amongst the Fathers . . . [he] quotes seven and twenty verses of the Erythraean Sibyl, which foretold the coming of Christ and his sufferings. His words are: 'He will fall into the hostile hands of the wicked; with poisonous spittle will they spit upon him; on the sacred back they will strike him; they will crown him with a crown of thorns; they will give him gall for food, and vinegar for drink. The veil of the temple will be rent, and at midday there will be a darkness of three hours long. And he will die, repose three days in sleep, and then, in the joyful light, he will come again as at first'." [10]

The Pyramids

Already we have learned much in searching the pyramids. Scientists have excavated, photographed, sorted, numbered, and named the artifacts unearthed. Others have measured the dimensions of the Great Pyramid and studied them in an effort to learn how humans could have constructed them with the limited function of ancient tools, and what the measurements might mean.

"As early as the eighteenth century the theory was already advanced that the Pyramid's base measurements were intentionally made to represent the number of days in the year. And in 1859, one John Taylor, a London mathematician and publisher, found other mathematical values in the structure and established the fact that the unit of measurement used was the Polar Diameter inch . . . the British and American inch of today . . . but Taylor also declared 'that the great pyramid was built to carry a divine revelation or prophecy'." [11]

Archangel Gabriel made mention of the fact that when humankind is prepared to understand it, more information will be found in the great pyramid.

Augury viewed as a science

5

"As time went by, augury became institutionalized in the Roman Republic, and augurs were gathered into a formal college . . . who administered pubic ceremonies and the keepers of the Sibylline books (a collection of ancient oracular prophecies)." [12]

Oracles
It is interesting to note that 'oracle' may refer to a holy site, a prophet who brings a message from a god, or the message itself.

"1 a. a person (as a priestess of ancient Greece) through whom a deity is believed to speak. b. a shrine in which a deity reveals hidden knowledge or the divine purpose through such a person. c. an answer or decision given by an oracle." [13]

'oracle' - "The answer given by certain divinities to inquiries of pilgrims coming to their shrines. The methods of expressing their reply varied; e.g., the rustling of the oak leaves at Dodona, the cries of the priestess at Delphi, the dreams at Epidaurus." [14]

It becomes evident that oracles laid the foundation in religion and spirituality. Over the centuries their messages changed in content, as explained by Ferm in his invaluable encyclopedia.

The spirituality of oracular messages
"The oracle is a new kind of ecstatic speech (in contrast to the meaningless babblings of the old ecstatics); it is intelligible, searching, morally profound, revealing behind phenomena the true spiritual situation and the immediate demand of Yahweh's holy will." [15]

". . . so-called 'supernatural' occurrences have been reported in all countries, and in all ages of the world's history . . . we may begin . . . when Greece was a flourishing and highly civilized nation. Belief in the supernatural powers of the Oracles was then all but universal – the most learned men accepting their utterances as 'divinely inspired' as completely as the unlettered and ignorant. How could this have been possible, if these oracular utterances had not been, at times, extraordinarily accurate?" [16]

Oracle of Delphi

"Delphi: ancient town in Greece on Mount Parnassus. Regarded as sacred for its oracle, a source of advice and moral teaching." [17]

As the patron of Delphi (*Pythian Apollo*), Apollo was an oracular god – the prophetic deity of the Delphic Oracle. Manas, in his *Divination*, provides details about the Delphic Oracle and her ritual of preparedness prior to channeling (in trance) the words of Apollo, God of Light.

"After careful purification she (Pythia, priestess of the shrine) sat on a tripod, a bowl on three legs, and fell into a trance-like state in which she received answers from Apollo. When she spoke, her words were copied down by a group of priests who then interpreted them and delivered the results to the supplicant.
". . . the oracle at Delphi was regarded as authoritative. It was consulted by anyone seeking guidance on major affairs of state, military expeditions, or religious or moral issues." [18]

This explanation indicates that the priests 'then interpreted' the words from Apollo. One might wonder why they required interpretation and on what basis the interpretation was made? Was the basis the priest's personal ego, or his specific religious beliefs, or something else?

We do not have any knowledge regarding the qualifications of the chosen pythia who channeled the words of Apollo. The only qualification we can be certain of is that she have the ability to so channel. This would require, then as now, a psychic ability to receive the words by inspiration or revelation.

Besides prophecy, sometimes the oracle gave other, unsolicited information, such as this comment about an historical figure:

". . . the Delphian oracle pronounced [Socrates] to be the wisest of mankind . . . who even today would care to deny that Socrates was correctly characterized by the oracle?" [19]

Although the oracles were respected and their prophecies considered sourced in a god, there is a record of one 'testing' of an oracular message. A story about testing the oracles is told by Herodotus:

"Croesus, King of Lydia, wished to make war on Cyrus, but feared to do so without the express sanction of Heaven. This was to be learned, of course, through the oracles. But it was first necessary to test the veracity of these. Accordingly, he dispatched envoys to six of the best known oracles then existing: those of Delphi, Dodona, Branchidae, Zeus Ammon, Trophonius, and Amphiaraus. On the hundredth day from their departure, the envoys were to ask these several oracles what was Croesus doing at home in Sardis at a *particular moment*. He had carefully kept the secret to himself, and had chosen an action which was beyond all possible conjecture.

"Four oracles failed; Amphiaraus was nearly right. Delphi alone   succeeded perfectly. This was the response, as given by Herodotus:

'I can count the sands, and I can measure the Ocean;

I have ears for the silent, and know what the dumb man meaneth;

Lo! On my sense there striketh the smell of a shell-covered tortoise,

Boiling now on a fire, with the flesh of a lamb, in a cauldron, ---

Brass in the vessel below, and brass the cover above it.' *Herodotus I: 21-25* [20]

For confirmation of the oracle's prophecy we provide the reader with this account (p. 31, Story of Psychic Science): "And what was Croesus actually doing at the time? We are told that 'on the departure of his messengers he had set himself to think what was most impossible for anyone to conceive of his doing, and then, waiting till the day agreed on came, he acted as he had determined. He took a tortoise and a lamb, and cutting them in pieces with his own hands, boiled them both together in a brazen cauldron, covered with a lid which was also of brass'."

Such guidance was often provided by the oracles, as well as telepathy and prophetic visions. "In other words, supernormal information was . . . obtained, very often, much as it is today." [21]

The foregoing story is a powerful example of the innate talent of the Delphic Oracle. No wonder rulers sought her guidance in matters regarding important decisions that had to be made without the benefit of a modern-day secret service group. However, the reader is reminded that Croesus ruled in 546 BCE, centuries *after* Saul, in the 11th Century BCE prohibited divination as evil. But then, Croesus was royalty.

CHAPTER 2
BEGINNING OF RECORDED HISTORY

1900-1100BCE

The Old Testament provides us with several examples of proscription of prophecy, at least for the general population. The prophets, on the other hand, were constantly receiving information and guidance from God. There is not an explanation in the Bible as to why necromancy was prohibited; it was simply stated and to be accepted as the law. What was the reason for condemnation of prophecy? Was it because it was seen as a pagan belief and the old prophets chose to disdain anything that was done by 'those pagans'? Or was it because the early church fathers were unable to prophesy as the pagans did? Or was it the belief that only those 'chosen by God' could prophesy? Yet it would appear that all the O.T. prophets were self-appointed.

The Encyclopedia of Religion (p.230) offers specific Old Testament examples of the proscription of divination: "divination by necromancy or evocation of ghosts was already prohibited by Saul in the 11th century B.C. (I Sam. xxviii, 3). Diviners of all kinds (Heb. *qosemim*) together with necromancers, sorcerers, interpreters of dreams and of clouds, were censured by the great prophets:
Mic. iii, 6-7
Is. ii, 6 . . .
Jer. xxvii, 9
Deut. xviii, 10, 14 . . .
Lev. xix, 26, 31, xx, 6, 27 etc."

Mesopotamia

Prior to the science of astronomy, astrology was the science. Once the separation was made, astrology was given a bad name. When astronomy was named as an accepted science, its findings were all based on scientific measurement and calculation. Astrology, instead, was based on the Zodiac, and thus fell into disrepute. ". . . by the 17thc both words took their current senses." [1]

It would be several centuries before science came into being. Some experimentation existed, but much of 'science' was learned only through revelation. What could be *seen*, such as the heavenly bodies, were observed and studied, their appearance and alteration of time recorded.

"Essentially, science was learned through divine 'revelation,' although it was also the object of experimental observation. . . The heavens, the world of the divinities, were painstakingly scrutinized. Periodic celestial phenomena, such as eclipses, were known and could be foretold. Still, the true Mesopotamian 'sciences' were divination and magic." [2]

World-wide we find races of men who sought to know the future and yet only a few of each race learned the talent of prophecy to fulfill that hunger.

In China, prior to 1000 B.C., "Shang Ti (Lord-on-High), an anthropomorphic god, lived in heaven and watched over the actions of the people, rewarding or punishing them for their deeds. . . To interpret heaven's will, priests resorted to divination. They carved grooves in tortoise shells or animal bones; then, after applying red-hot rods, they read the resulting cracks as messages from above." [3]

Clearly, only priests had the power of divination. It apparently was considered a talent bestowed by God Himself upon the religious leaders; inaccessible to the unlearned, untitled person --- and most of society at that time was uneducated.

8th and 7th Centuries BCE
Prior to biblical times prophecy was accepted universally, by studying the entrails of animals, clouds, wind, and the use of various tools such as dominoes, tea leaves, and playing cards. When we get to the Old Testament, however, many kinds of psychic phenomena are described. They also appear in the New Testament. These various kinds of phenomena are described in Part II herein. Also, see Appendix A

Divination practices included communication with the spirit world of the 'dead'. For there was an accepted belief in an afterlife. It is common knowledge that the Egyptians buried their dead – at least the royalty –with food, transportation and even their servants to help them after their death.

11

Etruscans
"People of ancient Italy [lived in]. . . . Etruria, region of their principal
settlements, [which] is north and west of the Tiber River (now
Tuscany). According to one explanation, they came from Lydia by sea
before 800B.C. . . . In [their] religion, nature worship, belief in an
afterlife, and the taking of auspices were important." [4]

Yet, Ferm, in his encyclopedia, describes these ancient prophets as
offering a new kind of divination. He devotes a full page to this topic,
including quotations from several books of the Old Testament.

"The classical prophets of the 8th and 7th cents. B.C. mark the
emergence of a new, unique quality in a movement with a long history
and lowly beginnings. Among their antecedents were the priestly
diviners, augurs, and seers who undertook to ascertain the divine will
and to forecast the future through instruments of divination, dreams
and induced ecstasy . . ." [5]

6th century BCE
The Babylonian Exile (about 600BCE) was prophesied centuries earlier
by Jeremiah in his Old Testament book. From Jeremiah, 50:2: *Declare ye
among the nations, and publish, and set up a standard; publish, and conceal not:
say, Babylon is taken, Bel is confounded, Merodach is broken in pieces; her idols
are confounded, her images are broken in pieces.*

Ancient Near East
"The connection between the two worlds, the visible and the invisible,
one conceived to the image of the other, was a fundamental conviction
in the Ancient Near East . . . The gods, who were powerful, intervened
in the world below; their enterprises and their actions were unforeseen,
but they were not always unforeseeable. Signs exist, which have to be
interpreted; suprahuman revelations can be coaxed from above and
utilized. Such was the basis of all forms of divination, which was so
widespread in the Ancient Near East." [6]

The phrase 'two worlds, the visible and the invisible' clearly supports
the idea of 'as above, so below' --- an ancient axiom. Revelations which
are 'coaxed from above' are, we now know, available to *all* humans,
in a meditative state.

5th century BCE

It is interesting to read the prophecies of various sibyls regarding Jesus the Christ, in detail, about his life and death experiences. The pictures painted by the verbiage of the sibyls were amazingly accurate and complete.

". . . The Erythraean Sibyl, . . . foretold the coming of Christ, and his sufferings. His words are: 'He will fall into the hostile hands of the wicked; with poisonous spittle will they spit upon him; on the sacred back they will strike him; they will crown him with a crown of thorns; they will give him gall for food, and vinegar for drink. The veil of the temple will be rent, and at midday there will be darkness of three hours long. And he will die, repose three days in sleep, and then, in the joyful light, he will come again as at first'." [7]

The Samian Sibyl . . .said, "That the Lord would be crowned with thorns and that He would have been given gall and vinegar to drink." [8]

In addition to a prophecy that Jesus would come, one sibyl also predicted the coming of John the Baptist:

The Persian Sibyl wrote: "When the time predicted shall come in which the Redeemer is to come into the world, the sound of a voice will be heard in the deserts, and that voice will invite mortals to prepare the way and cleanse their souls of vices and sins, and they will be baptized in pure and limpid waters". [9]

The sibyl who wrote most about Jesus was the Persian Sibyl. Most of her writings described his last days.

Persian Sibyl – "She has been painted 'with a book of her prophecies in the right hand and the left hand placed on her breast, the heavens illumined with a Cross in the center of the light, because she, more than all other Sibyls treated largely of the advent of the crucifixion of Christ our Lord. . ." [10]

It is easy for us, in this century, to read of the sibyls and compare them to modern psychics/mediums and their messages. Yet those ancient prophetesses were taken seriously by rulers, by saints and by popes. These historic figures took the oracles seriously regarding their prophetic ability, but also as laying the foundation for the Christian era which would follow:

"Among the Fathers of the Church who most upheld the oracles, stand pre-eminently the Pope Clement, Justin Martyr, Athenagoras, Theophilus of Antioch, Eusebius, Lantantius, Clement of Alexandria, St. Ambrose, Jerome, Augustin and Isidor of Seville, all of whom supported the truth of Christianity by the evidence of the Sibyls." [11]

3rd Century BCE: Druids

The druids were: "An order of men among the ancient celts of Gaul and Britain, who, according to Caesar, were priests, but in native Irish and Welsh legend, were magicians, soothsayers and the like".[12]

Sacrifice was included in many ancient beliefs. Animals and even humans, at times, were sacrificed in order to appease the various gods who were worshipped at the time. "The twin functions of divination and assuring the future were the most popular of the druids activities, and generally included some form of sacrifice." [13]

Nature provided all kinds of sources for the diviner, from heavenly bodies to birds and animals. Later, playing cards, dominos, and tea leaves were 'consulted'. Yet they all were merely focal points for the fortune teller. Modern psychics rely on direct communication with the spirit world, because they *know* that is the source and they also know that anyone has access to it.

"How can we know what fate has in store for us? Only by consulting druids, prophets or poets. Druids impressed Roman visitors with their ability to unlock the patterns of the future by observing the flight of birds, the phases of the moon or the movement of the stars." [14]

Various animals were also 'consulted', sometimes by observing their activities or by 'reading' the entrails of dead animals. "To foretell events was one such ability, and druids, bards and seers observed many animals in order to make divinations." [15]

Roman Empire

"Divination (from Latin *divinare* "to foresee, to be inspired by a god", related to *divinus*, divine) is the attempt to gain insight into a question or situation by way of a standardized process or ritual . . . Divination is often dismissed by skeptics, including the scientific community, as being mere superstition . . . most Romans believed in dreams and charms. From Wikipedia 10/11/10

From ancient times up to the Greeks and Romans more and more 'faith' was placed on natural events. "As Western cultures developed . . . divination became more formal. The early Greeks and Romans, for instance, assumed that almost every natural event was a sign from the gods." [16]

The heavens provided many 'signs' for seers. It is likely that since the gods and the heavens were both above and inaccessible to humans, the gods would use the activities of heavenly bodies to rule people.

"In ancient Rome, divination split into several distinct functions. Chief among these was augury. Regarded at the time as a profound science, augury was the study of eclipses as well as of thunder, the behavior of birds and animals, and other natural signs, called auspices. . . Since elections, consecrations, and declarations of war could be held in abeyance until they were augured auspicious, these seers exerted enormous control over the lives of citizens and the fates of communities." [17]

CHAPTER 3
BIBLICAL TIMES

Josephus is a book of the complete writings of Josephus, who lived from "A.D. 37 to sometime after A.D.100 . . . . [he] made a remarkable prophecy . . . that Vespasian would one day become Emperor. In itself, this was almost unthinkable, since the Julian (or Caesarean) line was still occupying the throne and no Emperor had yet been created outside of Rome. Who would have thought that less than a year later, Nero's suicide would bring the family of the Caesars to an end, or that two years later Vespasian would be named Emperor by his legions?" (William Sanford LaSor's Foreword to *Josephus*, viii).

Scripture

The word 'sibyl' does not appear in Scripture. It is possible that the sibyls of the ancient world were later called oracles, when some became famous in Greece and Italy. The word 'oracle' is found seventeen times in the Old Testament and 'oracles' four times in the New Testament. "Biblical prophecy, rich in poetry and beauty, among the very jewels of human literature, has moved and intrigued men for ages, and to this day new levels of meaning are constantly found in it." [1]

'New levels of meaning' are currently available to us, as we examine the parables from a metaphysical standpoint. An excellent source of information for the deeper meaning is *The Metaphysical Bible Dictionary*. Also, there are current books, channeled by Jesus himself, such as *New Teachings for an Awakening Humanity, Conversations with J.C.* and *A Course in Miracles*. Archangel Gabriel told us that *A Course in Miracles* will stand beside the Bible in importance in the centuries to come. These books provide us with what we are now ready to comprehend. The Holy Bible will never lose its holiness or its astounding literature, but as humanity evolves spiritually, the deeper meaning can be understood, appreciated, and applied to our daily life.

Belief in a devil, hell, and evil spirits permeated the mass consciousness since before biblical times. This stemmed from paganism, then mythology. The people's belief in, and fear of, a devil and hell became part of the Judeo-Christian Bible. ". . . the Old and New Testaments are full of stories of divination with low discarnate entities, or with high intelligences. They attribute these spiritualistic communications either to the devil and evil spirits, or to their God Jehovah Himself." [2]

If we accept the idea of a devil and a hell then we can readily accept the Bible and its stories of divination that include both. However, now that Archangel Gabriel has come to inform us that there is no devil -- nor hell – it is high time to review our belief system.

Anyone who honestly seeks to communicate with the spirit world of God knows that one must *first* ask that only 'good spirits' come through them. Without a place called 'hell' we must ask ourselves from where 'bad spirits' would come. Gabriel told us that there is a lower astral plane and a higher astral plane. Most of us will go to the higher astral. Entities on the lower astral can sway those on Earth only if earthlings seek their help, as Hitler did. It is also the reason that children, vulnerable to spirit influence, should never play with an Ouija board.

Those who live a life of negative behavior, hurting self and others, and who lack any faith in a higher power or will expect to go to 'hell', will find themselves in the lower astral plane. However it is only a temporary situation, as *every one of God's children will return unto God, our Father and our Source*. Gabriel explained that the original meaning of 'hell' (before the written word) was 'a shallow grave' --- because it was believed that wild animals would dig up their bones. Thus it became a curse.

Which plane one transitions to (at 'death'), depends on what one *expects* to find there. The lower astral is a dreary and barren place from which all can and do evolve to the higher astral *as they accept* the *fact that they are worthy* to do so. There are no fires of 'eternal damnation'. The higher astral is light, loving, peaceful and full of joy. There is no night there.

For all the scriptural proscriptions by the prophets against divination, there are some statements in the Bible which suggest that we not only ought to consult spirits, but also learn to discern which information is reliable and which is not. In Paul's first letter to the Thessalonians, he tells his readers:

17

Quench not the spirit.; Despise not prophesyings.; Prove all things; hold fast to that which is good. Thessalonians I: 19-21

Old Testament

A stunning example of physical phenomena is described in the book of Exodus. "Let us go back into sacred history. Do you know where the first lines were drawn concerning psychic phenomena? . . . It was when Moses was sent down into Egypt to deliver the Chosen People, and he was told to take the rod he had in his hand and – with Aaron, his brother – to go before Pharaoh. . . The magicians cast their rods down and they turned to serpents, too. But Aaron's rod or serpent ate up all the rest of them! . . . At this point, we can draw a dividing line between enchantments and the things of God." [3]

There are many prophets in the Old Testament. Were they divinely inspired or were they self-proclaimed? Probably at least some of them received information from God, but when a prophet speaks of killing others, we must accept the words as spurious, for God is Love and He could never suggest that one human being destroy another.

There are several definitions of Prophets in the Old Testament:
1. "A succession of Hebrew men of religion who claimed to be inspired by their God and to speak in his name, and whose claim is confirmed by the spiritual vitality and permanent worth of their work and message. . . ".[4]

2. In the OT, diviners are listed among influential men, together with "judges, prophets and elders". (Isaiah iii:2)

3. "The [OT] prophets were not forecasters or philosophers, but mystics, preachers, moralists, poets and men of action who felt themselves to be mouthpieces of Yahweh.(cf Exod. 4:14-16, 7:1) and instruments of Yahweh's creative purpose in man's historic life." [5]

During their sojourn across the desert, a pillar of fire and a pillar of cloud appeared to protect the Israelites, as told in Ex. 13:21 Archangel Gabriel told us that it was Archangel Metatron who formed these physical phenomena for the guidance required.

The Old Testament notes the oracle as a site, as well as a person. *"And against the wall of the house he [Solomon] built chambers round about, both of the temple and of the oracle; . . ."* I Kings 6:5 (also 20-21).

Nothing was more holy than the Ark of the Covenant and its placement would naturally be in the holy of holies in the temple. In I Kings 8:6 we find: *"And the priests brought in the ark of the covenant of the Lord unto his place, into the oracle of the house, to the most holy place, even under the wings of the cherubims".*

Solomon's temple and its departments compare with the Greek temples and its altar, where only priests and oracles could enter. "This innermost department of the temple of Solomon called the oracle, and the holy of holies, corresponds with the Adytum in the ancient Greek temples, where was the altar, and to which place only the priests and the Pythiae,or the prophetesses of Apollo had access." [6]

New Testament
Although the Bible does not mention numerology, another form of divination, Jakob Bohme, in his *Mysterium Magnum,* depicts Christ in a halo of numbers.[7]

St. Paul makes many references to supernatural events, such as: speaking in tongues, trance, angelic help and spirit guidance. See Appendix. One author sees Paul as totally immersed in supernatural experiences.

"If ever there was a manifestation of the supernatural, it was in the condition of things out of which arose the New Testament. We have only to take up the Epistles of St. Paul and we find him surrounded, penetrated, permeated with the supernatural. It is, as it were, the very atmosphere which he breathes. He does not assert it. He does not need to assert it. . . .St. Paul assumes it as a fact everywhere present to the consciousness of the readers as much as to his own." [8]

It is very interesting to note St. Peter's comment regarding God's oracles, and specifically the fact that he mentions 'any man'.

If any man speak, let him speak as the oracles of God; if any man minister, let him do it as of the ability which God giveth: that God in all things may be glorified through Jesus Christ, to whom be praise and dominion forever and ever. I Peter 4:11

History of Psychic Phenomena

There was a widespread use of divination of all known types among the ancient Greeks, Romans, Egyptians and Babylonians. "From this historical fact it is only logical to conclude that since Palestine was surrounded by these countries, its inhabitants, the Jews, were influenced by the practices of the neighboring nations." [9]

There is a plethora of examples of psychic phenomena in Scripture (see Appendix A for a complete list). Some examples are set forth here:

I Sam 8:7 and 8:22 – *'The Lord spoke to Samuel'* indicates that the prophet was clairaudient (is able to hear an entity living in the spirit world).

All oracles were not female, as revealed in the following:

In I Sam 9:6 – Saul speaks to his servant: *"Behold now, there is in this city a man of God, and he is an honourable man; all that he saith cometh surely to pass: now let us go thither; peradventure he can show us our way that we should go."*

Rulers not only had a firm belief in the diviners of the time, but openly spoke of them, at least to their servants.

I Sam. 28: 7 – *"Then said Saul unto his servant, Seek me a woman that hath a familiar spirit, that I may go to her, and enquire of her. And his servants said to him, Behold, there is a woman that hath a familiar spirit at Endor. "*

How interesting to note that King Saul knew of seers, and his servants were also privy to their existence. His servant had knowledge of the woman and her talent. We don't know if the lower class could afford a 'reading' from the woman at Endor, or if she charged on a 'sliding scale'.

Only rulers were privileged to have seers whom they consulted. Other seers worked in secret, for it was believed they must be tools of the devil.

"This woman seer [of Endor], due to the persecution of all mediums outside the officially recognized ones, the prophets, by the priesthood and by the king of Israel, was very careful for whom she should prophesy. . ." [10]

King David has his own seer, as we find in II Samuel.

II Sam. 24:11 – *"For when David was up in the morning, the word of the Lord came unto the prophet Gad, David's seer . . .".* This indicates that those in power accepted divination and hired their own personal seer.

II Kings 3:11 and 15-16 mention the existence of a *'prophet of the Lord'*

"The primary literary record of prophecy consists of oracles written down after oral utterance; these, as subsequently collected and edited along with narratives of the prophet concerned, and sometimes incorporating his memoirs (e.g., of Jeremiah) form the substantial nuclei of most of the prophetic books." [11]

In his 'law of God', Moses made specific mention of divination, ruled against its many expressions and separated them all from 'the spirit of prophecy' which God bestowed upon them. Anyone employing the several divination practices which he described, should be killed by stoning, a common death penalty at that time.

"Alexander Cruden, M.A. author of the Concordance to the Old and New Testament . . .

> The eastern people, and particularly the Israelites, were always very fond of divinations, magic, and the curious arts of interpretation dreams, and inquiring by unlawful methods into the knowledge of what was to come.
> This was a consequence of their timorous and superstitious genius. When Moses published the law of

God this evil was . . . very common in Egypt and the neighboring countries. To cure the Israelites of their inclination to consult diviners, fortune-tellers, augurs, and interpreters of dreams, etc. he gave them the promise of God, that the spirit of prophecy should not depart from them, and forbade them, under very severe penalties to consult diviners, astrologers and other persons of this kind. He commanded those who pretended to have a familiar spirit, or the spirit of divination, to be stoned." [12]

Examples of Mental Mediumship

Visions
Gen 15:1
After these things the word of the Lord came unto Abram in a vision, saying, Fear not, Abram: I am thy shield, and thy exceeding great reward.

Gen 46:2-4
And God spake unto Israel in the visions of the night, and said, Jacob, Jacob. And he said Here I am.
And he said, I am God, the God of thy father: fear not to go down into Egypt; for I will there make of thee a great nation:
I will go down with thee into Egypt; and I will also surely bring thee up again: and Joseph shall put his hand upon thine eyes.

Independent spirit voice
Matt 17:5
While he yet spake, behold, a bright cloud overshadowed them: and behold a voice out of the cloud, which said, This is my beloved Son, in whom I am well pleased; hear ye him.

Acts 10:13-16
And there came a voice to him, Rise, Peter; kill, and eat.
But Peter said, Not so, Lord; for I have never eaten anything that is common or unclean.

And the voice spake unto him again the second time, What God hath cleansed, that call not thou uncommon.

Examples of Physical Mediumship

Old Testament
Independent spirit writing
And he gave unto Moses, when he had made an end of communing with him upon the mount Sinai, two tables of testimony, tables of stone, written with the finger of God. Ex 31:18

Materialization
For the horse of Pharaoh went in with his chariots and with his horsemen into the sea, and the Lord brought again the waters of the sea upon them; but the children of Israel went on dry land in the midst of the sea. Ex 15:19

New Testament
And as they went to tell his disciples, behold, Jesus met them, saying, all hail. And they came and held him by the feet, and worshipped him. Matt 28:9

Then the same day at evening, being the first day of the week, when the doors were shut where the disciples were assembled for fear of the Jews, came Jesus and stood in the midst, and saith unto them, Peace be unto you. John 20:19

An event on the first Easter was described by Luke. He was the only apostle that noted this encounter with the risen Jesus: *And, behold, two of them [apostles] went that same day to a village called Emmaus . . .Jesus himself drew near, and went with them. But their eyes were holden that they should not know him.. . . And they drew nigh unto the village . .. they constrained him, saying, Abide with us: for it is toward evening, and the day is far spent.. . And it came to pass, as he sat at meat with them, he took bread, and blessed it, and brake, and gave to them. And their eyes were opened, and they knew him; and he vanished out of their sight.* Luke24:13-31.

Inspirational speaking,

23

But when they shall lead you, and deliver you up, take no thought beforehand what ye shall speak, neither do ye premeditate: but whatsoever shall be given you in that hour, that speak ye: for it is not ye that speak, but the Holy Ghost. Mark 13:11

Independent spirit voice
Father, glorify thy name. Then came there a voice from heaven, saying, I have both glorified it, and will glorify it again.
The people therefore, that stood by, and heard it, said that it thundered: others said, An angel spake to him.
Jesus answered and said, This voice came not because of me, but for your sakes. John 12:30

Healing of magnetized articles
And God wrought special miracles by the hands of Paul:
So that from his body were brought unto the sick handkerchiefs or aprons, and the diseases departed from them, and the evil spirits went out of them. Acts 19:11-12

The Bible as a Learning Tool

Scripture contains a grand statement made by Jesus Christ: *Verily, verily, I say unto you, He that believeth on me, the works that I do shall he do also; and greater works than these shall he do; because I go unto my Father.* John 14:12 I cannot imagine what 'greater works' could be done by believers, but the message is clear – that what Jesus did then can be done by anyone who believes in him. This confirms other passages in the Bible that refer to Jesus as an example and a way-shower.

"If the reader will trust to his own indwelling Spirit of truth for light, he will find in these suggestions a guide to endless inspiration in the understanding of Truth. . . We are always pleased when any one learns to go within and get his inspiration direct from his own indwelling Lord or Spirit of truth. " [13]

When we search the Bible for instruction in divination, we find that there is an inconsistency regarding its use, its users, and its benefits.

"The attitude of the Bible toward divination is decidedly ambivalent. On the one hand, verses like Deuteronomy 18:10-12 clearly forbid any acts of divination, describing them as something detestable to God. On the other hand Exodus 28 gives members of the priestly class the authority to perform divinatory rituals inside the temple. . . . Divination appears to be condoned in several places in the Hebrew Bible such as the chastisement of Noah, the journey of the sons of Jacob to Egypt, and the selection of a king by Samuel. It appears not so much that divination is forbidden in the Bible, but its use was restricted to people whom God appointed. " [14]

"However personal his [Amos] words may be, they form part of a tradition; they enter into a movement of prophetic inspiration that was evident already." (p.109, *The Formation of the Bible*) This is a clear reference to divination. What else could 'prophetic inspiration be?"

A clear distinction is made between 'true prophecy' and various kinds of divination, even though prophecy *is a form of divination.*

From Moses on, biblical leaders rejected divination of any kind, at least for the masses. "Divination and related practices are rejected as alien to true prophecy after the fashion of Moses (Deut 9:18-22)." [15]

Yet, scripture is full of various kinds of divination. "The Bible, both the Old and New Testaments, is full of . . . stories of spiritualistic séances in which the various prophets, diviners, or mediums prophesied for these people, as are the records of any other people of ancient times." [16]

The Tower of Babel was prophesied by a sibyl. We find in Josephus (book 1, ch.4, sec. 3):
"The Sibyl also makes mention of this tower, and of the confusion of the language, when she says thus: 'When all men were of one language, some of them built a high tower, as thereby they would ascend up to heaven; but the gods sent storms of wind and overthrew the tower, and gave everyone his peculiar language; and for this reason it was that the city was called *Babylon*."

The Apocrypha

One definition of apocrypha: "books included in the Septuagint and Vulgate but excluded from the Jewish and protestant canons of the Old Testament" [17]

Another definition of apocrypha: "Although not scriptural they claimed to preserve visions granted to holy men, and could thus be regarded as in some sense of divine origin." [18]

The apocryphal books, written in the first two centuries, were not included in the official canon of the church because they were not considered 'authentic.' Because of the exquisite details of the writings, it is difficult to believe that they were considered spurious.

This author takes exception to the early church leaders who chose to omit the apocryphal books from the official canon. I base this on the fact that they contain detailed descriptions, including the birth of Jesus and his early childhood. The so-called 'hidden' books of the Bible include a lovely passage in which the mother of the Virgin Mary was also divinely conceived:

"Be not afraid, Joachim, nor troubled at the sight of me, for I am an angel of the Lord sent by him to you, that I might inform you, that your prayers are heard . . . when [God] shuts the womb of any person, he does it for this reason, that he may in a more wonderful manner again open it, and that which is born appear to be not the product of lust, but the gift of God . . . Anna your wife shall bring you a daughter, and you shall call her name Mary". Gospel of the birth of Mary II: 3-9 [19]

Jesus the Christ
From his virgin birth on, and through every phase of his life, Jesus was an exceptionally psychic person. He spoke while in his cradle.

"The following accounts we found in the book of Joseph the high-priest, called by some Caiaphas:

He relates, that Jesus spake even when he was in the cradle, and said to his mother:

Mary, I am Jesus the Son of God, that word which thou didst bring forth according to the declaration of the angel Gabriel to thee, and my father hath sent me for the salvation of the world." The Gospel of the birth of Mary I: 1-3 [20]

An example of fire mediumship is found in the following passage, regarding Jesus' baby clothes which failed to burn in the fire.

". . . they produced the swaddling cloth which St. Mary had given to them . . . according to the custom of their country, made a fire, they worshipped it.

And casting the swaddling cloth into it, the fire took it, and kept it.

And when the fire was put out, they took forth the swaddling cloth unhurt, as much as if the fire had not touched it." First Gospel of the Infancy of Jesus Christ, III:5-8 [21]

The healing of magnetized articles is described as follows, when Jesus' clothes in infancy provided healing to the sick.

The son answered, When the devils seized me, I went into the inn, and there found a very handsome woman with a boy, whose swaddling clothes she had just before washed, and hanged out upon a post.

One of these I took, and put it upon my head, and immediately the devils left me, and fled away. First Gospel of the Infancy of Jesus Christ, IV: 19-20 [22]

As a young person, Jesus foretold his relationship with the robbers on either side of him at the crucifixion.

In their journey from hence thy came into a desert country, and were told it was infested with robbers; so Joseph and St. Mary prepared to pass through it in the night.

. . . behold they saw two robbers . . . Titus and Dumachus; and Titus said to Dumachus, I beseech thee let those persons go along quietly, that our company many not perceive anything of them:

. . . When the Lady St. Mary saw the kindness which this robber did shew them, she said to him, The Lord God will receive thee to his right hand, and grant thee pardon of thy sins.

Then the Lord Jesus answered, and said to his mother, When thirty years are expired, O mother, the Jews will crucify me at Jerusalem;

And these two thieves shall be with me at the same time upon the cross, Titus on my right hand, and Dumachus on my left. . . First Gospel of the Infancy of Jesus Christ VIII: 1-7 [23]

27

Jesus was the son of God and expressed that love continually, but not flamboyantly. "It was evident that a unique relationship existed between God and himself [Jesus]; they carried on an almost uninterrupted communication, although its exterior manifestations were simple and unspectacular. Men received the impression that no one else had ever loved God, or 'known' him in a religious experience, as Jesus did – so spontaneously, so continually, to such a high degree, and with such interior purity. His whole religion was to 'do the will of the Father'." [24]

Materialization (when a spirit entity becomes visible to the mortal eye). An example of materialization is provided in Matt. 17:1-5 when Elias and Moses both were seen by Peter, James and John as they met with Jesus on the mountain.

St. Paul was a trance medium, as noted in Acts 22:17: "*And it came to pass, that, when I was come again to Jerusalem, even while I prayed in the temple, I was in a trance. . .*"

Peter also 'fell into a trance' in Acts 10:10-19 "*And he became very hungry, and would have eaten: but while they made ready, he fell into a trance.*"

For the individual accepting only a literal view of Scripture, there are undeniable references to the encouragement of humans seeking communication with spirit:

Quench not the Spirit. I Thess: 19
Despise not prophesyings. I Thess: 20
If any man speak, let him speak as the oracles of God . . . I Peter 4:11
*Try the spirits whether they are of God. . .*I John 4:1

CHAPTER 4
FIRST TO FIFTEENTH CENTURIES

1ˢᵗ Century
Even after biblical times, divination was still condemned.
"In 692 the Quinisext Council, also known as the Council in Trullo in
the Eastern Orthodox Church, passed canons to eliminate pagan and
divination practices".[1]

4ᵗʰ Century
The conversion of Constantine
"Constantine the Great, in 330 A.D. ordered removal of the sacred
tripod of the Pythia, the statue of Apollo . . . the Muses and . . . Pan
and [had them] taken to Constantinople." [2]

> Perhaps the most famous prophetic dream in history
> was that bestowed upon Constantine in 312 as he
> prepared to invade Rome and claim the throne of
> Emperor Maxentius. The night before the great battle
> an angel appeared in Constantine's dreams bearing the
> Chi-Rho monogram of Christ. 'By this conquer,'
> directed the angel. Accordingly, Constantine's men
> went into combat with the emblem on their shields, and
> Maxentius obligingly made the dumbest military move
> of his life (never fight with your back to a river).
> Thunderstruck, Constantine called his advisers together
> and inquired which god was represented by the sign.
> Finding that it was the symbol of Christ, Constantine
> promptly converted, and with him, Europe.[3]

But later in that century the Emperor of Rome attempted revival of the
Delphic Oracle.
"A few years later (361-363) Julian the Apostate, the Roman Emperor,
tried to revive the Oracle at Delphi . . . He sent a famous physician as
his emissary, but he brought back to the emperor the following:
'Tell the king, the fair-wrought hall has fallen to the ground. No longer
has Phoebus a hut, nor a prophetic laurel, nor spring that speaks. The
water of speech even is quenched'." [4]

Jesus himself predicts the end of prophecy as given by the oracle at Delphi.

The End of Oracular Prophecy

Jesus predicts end of the Delphic Oracle.

> The Delphic sun has set; the Oracle will go into decline; the time is near when men will hear its voice no more.
>
> The gods will speak to man by man. The living Oracle now stands within these sacred groves; the Logos from on high has come.
>
> From henceforth will decrease my wisdom and my power; from henceforth will increase the wisdom and the power of him Immanuel . . .
>
> And Jesus said, 'It is not angel, man, nor god that speaks. It is the matchless wisdom of the master minds of Greece, united in a master mind.
>
> This giant mind has taken to itself the substances of soul, and thinks, and hears, and speaks.
>
> It will remain a living soul while master minds feed it with thought, with wisdom and with faith and hope.
>
> But when the master minds of Greece shall perish from the land, this giant master mind will cease to be, and then the Delphic Oracle will speak no more'. [5]

Although the oracle at Delphi, the most famous of all the oracles, came to an end, it predicted that 'the gods will speak to man by man'; which means that humankind will learn from God through the methods of psychism and mediumship. Prophecy has always existed and probably always will, as long as humans seek to know. And the curiosity of all people, it seems, is insatiable.

Some writers see the end of prophecy as occurring after the exile. The 'exile' refers to the time (597 – 538 B.C.E.) when the Babylonians, under the rule of Nebuchadnezzar, captured and deported to Babylonia a large group of Judeans. Scriptural sources differ as to the number of Jews deported to Babylonia Some mention 20,000 as a minimum number.

"In my view, then, we cannot correctly say that prophecy ended with the exile, either in the sense that it ceased or that it was transformed into something else. . . we ought to conceive of prophecy as a continuing potentiality in a given society, based on that society's particular religious beliefs and past experience. This view allows for the intermittent appearance of prophets within the society and defines the conditions under which prophecy can be said to end, as well as begin again . . ." [6]

The Bible is full of prophecy and the lives of prophets. Prophecy has not diminished 2000 years later, in and out of Christianity.
"For all the talk of its demise, the notion of prophecy is by no means absent from contemporary Christian discourse. Paul Hanson, who believes that prophecy as such came to an end in the early postexilic period, claims that prophetic 'activity' is recognizable in the early church, at the time of the Protestant Reformation, and even today." [7]

7th Century
Divination was considered a pagan practice in the early Christian church. Later the church would pass canon laws forbidding the practice of divination. In 692 the Quinisext Council, known as the Council in Trullo in the Eastern Orthodox Church, passed canons to eliminate pagan and divination practices. [8]

9th Century
"In the 9th century witches were burned alive." [9]

11th-16th Century Saints
Prophecy maintained its importance due to the fact that many saints were prophetic. They thus had protection due to their status.

> "Saints . . . generally had an easier time with their
> prophesying. Perhaps it was because females could

never aspire to the papal chair; possibly because
Sibylline utterance is natural to women; or it may be for
reasons of chivalry. In any case, women with some
notable exceptions, were universally welcomed as
prophets, and usually received the recognition and
respect of the highest authority of the church. Saints
such as Hildegarde, of Bingen, in the twelfth century,
St. Mechtild of Magdeburg in the thirteenth, and Sts.
Catherine and Birgitta in the fourteenth, were not only
listened to, but received high homage and profound
deference during their lifetimes, and that naturally made
the way to later canonization comparatively easy for
them." [10]

Prophecy usually contained information of guidance as well as future
happenings. One saint dared to prophesy about the papal throne.

St.Malachi._"In the year 1139 [Malachi] undertook a journey to Rome
to visit Pope Innocent III, and on the way . . . he wrote down his
famous prophecy concerning the popes." [11]

Hildegard of Bingen_A twelfth century nun, "Immured from the age of
eleven in a small nunnery on the Rhine . . . became famous for her
visions and ensuing edicts. According to the pictures she bid her
faithful scribe to draw, the spirit came down on her head in tongues of
flame and she wrote the words it told her. She was consulted by
peasants and lords for miles around . . ." [12]

Joan of Arc (1412-1431). "Perhaps history's most famous clairaudient
[hearing things not perceptible to human ears] was Joan of Arc . . .
    "A medieval peasant, Joan lived in a world far less visual than
ours.

    "Joan said she first heard the voices when she was thirteen. They
belonged, she said, to Saints Michael, Margaret and Catherine, and
carried messages from God, directing her destiny and foretelling her
future" [13]

Because so much has been written about Joan of Arc, the life she lived
and the power she derived from spirit at such an early age, she has

remained famous to all future generations. "She came, with powers and genius which should be the marvel of the world while the world stands. She redeemed a nation, she wrought such works as seemed to her people, and well might seem, miraculous. . . " [14]

Condemnation of divination resumes
However, soon after Joan of Arc died, the pope issued a pronouncement against 'witches'. Not only those who prophesied, but even those who predicted the weather!

Only six years after Joan of Arc died, a papal bull (official letter) was issued:
"In 1437 and 1445, Pope Eugene IV issued bulls commanding punishment of witches who caused bad weather, and in 1484 the bull *Summis Desiderantes*, by Pope Innocent VIII, started a wave of torture and execution in which many scores of thousands were killed. Similar bulls were issued by Julius II and Adrian VI. Nor did the Reformation put an end to the terror. Luther joined in the denunciation of witches and there were many executions in protestant Scotland in the seventeenth century." [15]

The strongest condemnation of 'witchcraft' came from Pope Innocent VIII, when he supported a writing entitled *Witches Hammer*, a book containing detailed steps in how to torture and kill those who dared to prophesy or even deny that demons existed. This author held an English translation of the *Witches Hammer* at a used book store in Saratoga County, New York. I felt a strong desire to replace it on the shelf and to not even put it in my home bookcase.

The Aztecs
"Sorcery had become partly professionalized by the Aztec era (14th-5th centuries) . . .
"The greatest demand was for diviners – a role partly filled by the priests who specialized in interpreting the 260 day almanac. Other individuals read the future in the patterns maize grains formed when scattered on a cloak. Fortune tellers – often old women – would gaze into pots of water or mirrors of polished obsidian in search of clues . . . " [16]

Gazing into a shiny surface is called scrying, and it was the method used by Nostradamus in obtaining his quatrains of prophecy.

The Renaissance

South American oracles

Throughout later centuries other cultures accepted oracles, often outdoors rather than sequestered in a holy building.

In the 17th century a priest researched and wrote *History of the New World.* . . .
"Among the first objects of the Spaniards' attentions were the oracles: holy sites to which rulers and commoners alike would go for advice on important questions or to learn what the future had in store. In a world in which natural features were frequently imbued with numinous [supernatural, holy, spiritual] powers, oracles were commonly in the open air." [17]

The power of oracles was widespread. The oracles of Peru were so highly regarded that even invaders from Spain feared for themselves if they harmed the site of the oracle at Pachacamac.

"But the greatest of all the Andean oracles lay at Pachacamac, not far from modern-day Lima. Its reputation long pre-dated the Incas, who did not dare to tamper with it when they conquered the region in the late fifteenth century." [18]

Peru had its own oracles, near today's Lima, who received messages from the god in whom they believed. ". . . the oracle . . . was located in a chamber atop a stepped adobe-brick pyramid. The god who resided there not only offered advice to individuals, including the Inca emperor, but was also reputedly able to provide protection against bad weather, crop failure, earthquakes, and disease." [19]

In France, the king's bishop foretold 'upheavals and transformations' with wide ranging effects, but did not give any details. He only mentioned the possibility that the world might not exist much longer.

"Pierre d'Ailly, born about 1350, was Chancellor of the University of Paris ... almoner to the King of France, Bishop of Cambray, a cardinal ... what he wrote of 1789 was this: 'Should the world still remain in existence at that time, which God alone knows, then astounding upheavals and transformations will occur which will effect our laws and political structure.'"

Mother Shipton (1448)
One of the most unusual predictions ever written was offered in poetic form. Events impossible to know, or even understand, were foretold by Mother Shipton. They have all been realized by modern man.

This extraordinary Englishwoman and seer wrote the following:
>Carriages without horses will go,
>And accidents fill the world with woe.
>Around the earth thoughts shall fly
>In the twinkling of an eye;
>The world upside down shall be,
>And gold be found at the root of a tree.
>Through hills man shall ride,
>And no horse be at his side.
>Under water men shall walk,
>Shall ride, shall sleep, shall talk.
>In the air men shall be seen
>In white, in black, in green;
>Iron in the water shall float,
>As easily as a wooden boat.
>Gold shall be found and shown
>In a land that's not yet known.
>Fire and water shall wonders do,
>England shall at last admit a foe.
>The world to an end shall come
>In eighteen hundred and eighty-one.[20]

CHAPTER 5
SIXTEENTH TO EIGHTEENTH CENTURIES

Nostradamus (1503-1566)

It would be difficult to over-emphasize the importance of Nostradamus. Today he still commands much attention, as noted in current TV programs. "The most celebrated prophet who has ever appeared in Europe, possibly the most celebrated outside the Bible, was Michael Nostradamus . . . It is safe to say that in all European history there was no one who stands out more for the . . . unusual gifts of clairvoyance than does this Provencal physician and seer . . . a man who could conquer the great plagues of his time, yet was a humble worshipper of God, and also the greatest prophet of his age and all subsequent ages." [1]

One of the Nostradamus stanzas and its manifestations:
> "The young lion will conquer the old one upon the
> field in single combat. He will pierce his eyes in a
> golden cage, who will then die a dreadful death. . .

> "Nostradamus was a contemporary of King Henry II
> of France. In July 1559, King Henry celebrated the
> marriage of his sister . . . as part of the festivities held a
> magnificent tournament . . . invited one of his guests,
> the young Earl of Montgomery, of the Scots Guard, to
> cross lances with him in the tourney. The young north
> Briton modestly declined this too great and too
> dangerous honor. The King, however, insisted, and in
> the heat of the tilting the Earl's lance pierced the
> golden visor of his opponent's helmet, entered his right
> eye, and Henry II died soon thereafter a horribly
> painful death." [2]

Interpretation of Nostradamus' writings continues to challenge us. Usually they can only be understood after the fact. Some have still not been interpreted, possibly because their predictions have not as yet manifested on earth.

"Of the thousand or so of [Nostradamus'] quatrains (Ten Centuries) not nearly all have been deciphered and interpreted. . ." wrote Forman in 1940. [3] The tool that Nostradamus used for his prophecies was scrying. "Possibly the most pervasive form of natural divination is known as scrying, in which a practitioner presumes to plumb the depths of hidden knowledge by concentrating on a smooth, clear or reflective surface . . ." [4]

However, the crystal ball has won over many mediums as their 'tool of choice'.

The commonest form of divination is probably crystal ball gazing'. . . no scrying tool outdoes the alleged power of the . . . crystal ball. And no crystal gazer has cut a more dramatic swath through history than the Englishman John Dee -- mathematician, philosopher, and adviser to Queen Elizabeth I." [5]

But punishment persisted for those who dared to prophesy. They all did so at their peril.

"Soothsaying and forms of divination were widespread through the Middle Ages. In the constitution of 1572 and public regulations of 1661 of Kur-Saxony, capital punishment was used on those predicting the future." Wikip. But in West Africa prophecy was accepted publicly and fortune-tellers sold their services in the open market place:

"Sixty miles south of the river Niger . . . a West African tribe called the Dogon has endured for more than four centuries . . . the Dogons rely on ancient methods of divination to render the critical decisions affecting their tribe . . . village fortune-tellers sit alongside purveyors of meats and spices . . . For a few coins they will shake a handful of cowrie shells into a straw basket and read the customer's future in the patterns." [6]

17th Century

There is not only a persistence of belief in prophecy, but many authors make mention of it. Forman, in *The Story of Prophecy* notes, "For, notwithstanding skepticism and ridicule, prophecy is a phenomenon that for thousands of years has sunk deep roots into the consciousness of humanity, and fails to be eradicated." [7]

Some prophecies address issues in the near future; others reach far into time, such as: ". . . Francis Bacon . . . foretold flying and submarines." [8]

To identify the year, or even the century, when prophecy began, it must have had roots in mythology – the stories which the ancients have handed down through time.

From mythology of SW Nigeria, Africa, we find: "Ile-Ife occupied a special place in Yoruba myth as a spot where Earth was created. Oduduma, who was sent down from the heavens, to accomplish the task, went on to found the city itself. When the *orishas* - the sky-dwelling gods of Yoruba legend – saw that his work was good, they came down to inspect it. One was Orunmila, who taught people the art of divination and founded the city of Benin." [9]

Even into the 17th century, legislative bodies took some prophecy very seriously. Stellar (of the stars) prophecy was accepted, in addition to the possibility of yet another hidden source of knowledge.

"The English astrologer William Lilly foretold in the year 1651 the London plague of 1665 . . . and the London fire of 1666. So comparatively accurate was this prediction, that a Parliamentary commission examined Lilly to question him as to whether any knowledge other than stellar had inspired his prophecy." [10]

Some prophecies seemed impossible to ever come true. And yet Mr. Peare predicted an unprecedented, succession to the throne of England: "Another Englishman, A. J. Peare, prophesied in 1868, when the late King George was only a two-year-old infant and had older brothers living, that he should be King of England under the title of George V." [11]

From ancient times to the time of scripture, prohibitions against prophecy – called witchcraft -- pertained. In biblical times several prophets condemned it. *The Witches Hammer*, by the Roman Catholic Church, gave detailed instructions on how to torture and murder those who predicted the future. The middle ages saw constant persecution and only in the 18th century were laws enacted to end this terrible and unfounded torture.

18th Century

Though the practice of witchcraft has existed all over the world from ancient times, the most extensive witchcraft persecution in the modern world began in Europe about the close of the Middle Ages and lasted until the eighteenth century. During the late seventeenth century it found echoes in the well-known trials of Salem, Massachusetts, and elsewhere in the American colonies.[12]

Germany had its own famous seers who wrote volumes of prophecy, which proved to be true. They were not rulers nor did they serve the Church, proving that divination is not an art assigned to royalty or God's servants.

"There is a voluminous prophetic literature in the Reich . . . two of Germany's most outstanding seers, highly confirmed and authenticated by research . . . were Christian Heering, a Saxon fisherman, and Johann Adam Muller, a farmer near Heidelberg." [13]

Swedenborg (1688-1772)

Today, it seems, relatively few people have heard of Emanuel Swedenborg. Yet the concordance of his writings fills fifteen volumes! After devoting many years to scientific research and writing the results, he had an amazing experience which turned his time and attention to theological lessons he had learned through experiences on the other side – the Heaven world.

W. F. Prince, in his book *Noted Witnesses for Psychic Occurrences*, (pp.46-55), four instances of Swedenborg's experiences are given. One, probably the most well-known, is the day that he 'saw' in his mind's eye, a fire near his home in Stockholm while having dinner at a friend's home in Gottenberg (300 miles distant). Three days later the fire, its specific destruction, and the time of its extinguishment all precisely agreed with Swedenborg's vision.

Immanuel Kant gathered information regarding the fire and reported it the same. [14] But apparently another experience, more profound and alarming, was a vision Swedenborg had in his later years:

"In 1745, at the age of fifty-seven, Swedenborg had an experience that radically changed the course of his life. Much later, he would describe it as a vision of Jesus Christ commissioning him to 'open to people the spiritual meaning of Scripture' and initiating years of regular experiences of the spiritual world. Soon after this vision, he resigned from his post on the Swedish Board of Mines and spent the remainder of his years writing and publishing the theological works for which he is now best known." [15]

This was probably the very first time that the term 'spiritual meaning of scripture' was introduced into the English language and psyche. Now, those who insisted on only the literal meaning of the Bible had to revise the 'old time religion' idea. There is one thing above all else that confirms the validity of communication with the spirit realm. That one thing is consistency. Over the period of many years Swedenborg claims that he constantly and without interruption spent time 'in the company' of angels and spirits.

It is hard to believe that Swedenborg actually conversed with angels and spirits, yet he experienced this communication over several years. Our benefit, nearly three centuries later, is that he put the experiences in writing.

"It may therefore be stated in advance that of the Lord's Divine mercy it has been granted me now for some years to be constantly and uninterruptedly in company with spirits and angels, hearing them speak and in turn speaking with them. [16]

In some individuals who have the gift of prophecy or spirit communication, the talent surfaces at a very young age. Others are trained in using their innate psychic ability. Yet others, like Swedenborg, have a unique experience, as an adult, in which the talent is revealed in a moment of revelation.

". . . He [Swedenborg] devoted himself to scientific studies and philosophical reflections . . . From 1743 to 1745 he entered a transitional phase. . . science and philosophy to theology. Throughout the rest of his life he maintained that this shift was brought about by Jesus Christ, who appeared to him, called him to a new mission, and opened his perception to a permanent dual consciousness of this life and the life after death." [17]

In accepting the idea of 'dual consciousness' we acknowledge the truth of our being: at *all times* we have a consciousness of our earthly life and surroundings *and* a consciousness which is eternal – that spirit self of us which is sourced in God. It must be impossible to describe a personal experience with angels, or to tell another in feeble words what Heaven is like, after visiting it. But we are blessed with some feeble words of Swedenborg when he attempts to tell us of his experience.

> ". . . The idea at once struck me how great the grace of the Lord is, who accounts and appropriates to us our resistance to temptation, though it is purely God's grace and is His and not our work; and He overlooks our weaknesses in it, which yet must be manifold . . . Afterward I awoke and slept again many times and all was in answer to my thoughts, yet so that in everything there was such life and glory that I can give no description of it; for it was all heavenly, clear to me at the time, but afterward inexpressible. In short I was in heaven, and I heard a language which no human tongue can utter with its inherent life, nor the glory and inmost delight resulting from it. Besides, while I was awake I was in a heavenly ecstasy which is also indescribable. . . Praise and honor and glory be to the Highest! Hallowed be His Name! Holy, Holy, Lord God of Hosts!" [18]

When such a revelation comes, how can it help but change one's direction in life? Divine guidance impels us all to use our gifts of communication and writing to announce to others the exquisite experience of spirit communication. We approach the inspired task with a new zeal and thank God for the heavenly experience. We also thank God that our words may inspire others and help them derive confidence and faith in the God of their understanding.

". . . From that day I gave up the study of all worldly science and labored in spiritual things, according as the Lord opened my eyes, very often daily, so that in midday I could see into the other world, and in a state of perfect wakefulness converse with angels and spirits." [19]

In addition to his unique gift of conversing with those in the spirit world, Mr. Swedenborg also was given predictions about the future.

"In the year 1762, on the very day when Peter III of Russia died, Swedenborg . . . said, "Now, at this very hour, the Emperor Peter III has died in prison --- explaining the nature of his death . . . The papers soon after announced the death of the Emperor, which had taken place on the very same day." [20]

We can thank Mr. Swedenborg for a clear statement about our 'death' experience. Now we call it 'transition', since there is no death. "According to Swedenborg, the transition to immortal life is rapid, easy, and without shock; he declared that he had conversed with at least 'an hundred thousand' in the other world who had been dead for differing periods, ' of whom many were in heaven and many in the hells. . . . " [21]

Swedenborg's writings are still available from the Swedenborg Foundation in Pennsylvania He has influenced generations since his death and will influence generations to come as people accept the idea that humans can communicate with the spirit world of God. It is not common knowledge that Helen Keller was inspired by his writings, and her own writing is available from the Swedenborg Foundation.

"Just six years after Swedenborg's death a Viennese doctor, Anton Mesmer, arrived in Paris – creating a furor by his teachings and his cures. He seemed to possess a remarkable power, -- placing his subjects in a trance-like condition, in which state many extraordinary phenomena were alleged to have occurred." [22] This was the beginning of what is now known as Mesmerism. Out of Mesmerism came Hypnotism, named by Dr. James Braid in 1842.[23]

Goethe
In c. 1771 Goethe, poet and dramatist, had 'A PREDICTIVE VISION':

> I now rode on horseback over the footpath to
> Drusenheim, when one of the strangest experiences
> befell me. Not with the eyes of the body, but with

those of the spirit, I saw myself on horseback coming toward me on the same path dressed in a suit such as I had never worn, pale-grey with some gold. As soon as I had shaken myself out of this reverie the form vanished. It is strange, however, that I found myself returning on the same path eight years afterward to visit Fredericka once more and that I then wore the suit I had dreamt of, and this not by design but by chance. Be this as it may, the strange phantasm had a calming influence on my feelings in those moments following the parting.[24]

Many prophets had predicted the coming of the French Revolution. In the sixteenth century two individuals gave such prophecy.

"The [French] Revolution had been predicted during hundreds of years. Pierre d'Ailly, Bishop of Cambray . . . foretold it four centuries before. . Turrel . . . in 1531. In a book with a long title published at Lyons in 1550, Richard Rousset . . . gives it as the universal agreement of all astrologers of that time." [25]

Mother Ann Lee
Ann Lee was founder of the Shakers in America. Her acceptance of the Christ directing her thoughts is expressed in this phrase: "It is not I that speak, it is Christ who dwells in me. I converse with Christ; I feel him present with me, as sensibly as I feel my hands together." [26]

CHAPTER 6
NINETEENTH CENTURY: NEW AGE BEGINS

The ages of human life on Earth are best described by Levi in the Introduction to his *The Aquarian Gospel of Jesus the Christ*. Briefly, there exists a Central Sun, around which our universe revolves. One revolution takes approximately 24,000 years, and divided into Zodiac segments, every 2000 years we enter a new age. Jesus came at the beginning of the age of Pisces – hence the fish to denote his presence or memory. Now are we entering the Age of Aquarius. Archangel Gabriel is the announcer of the ages. He told us this is the Age of Truth.

Nineteenth Century
"new age":"An eclectic group of cultural attitudes arising in late 20th century Western society that are adapted from those of a variety of ancient and modern cultures, that emphasize beliefs (as reincarnation, holism, pantheism and occultism) outside the mainstream, and that advance alternative approaches to spirituality, right living, and health." [1]

To differ with Webster, the New Age began in the mid-19th Century when several religious beliefs blossomed forth at the time in the United States, such as Spiritualism (Fox sisters), Mormonism (Church of Latter Day Saints, founded by Joseph Smith, Jr.), Church of Divine Science (Nona Brooks), Quakers (George Fox), Church of Religious Science (Ernest Holmes), Unity Church (Myrtle and Charles Fillmore).

Joseph Smith claimed that an angel gave him gold plates with inscriptions, which translated resulted in the Book of Mormon. Mother Myrtle and Charles Fillmore healed themselves by studying Scripture and talking to their body.

To this writer, the most astounding example of spirit communication is a book entitled *The Voice Celestial*, by Ernest Holmes. I am convinced that it is a channeled work (from spirit) for the following reasons:

1. It is the antithesis of Holmes' earlier writings which are pragmatic in approach.

2. Holmes wrote very little poetry and it did not compare in style with *The Voice Celestial*. To present the information in this book in poetry style seems to me an example of supreme literary expertise.

3. Holmes never wrote about the history of religion nor did his writings imply that others should. Yet *The Voice Celestial* brings the reader from ancient times to the present.

The middle of the nineteenth century we had the first stirrings of New Age thinking, which included the concept that women were equal to men in society, entitled to all the same rights and privileges that men had possessed for centuries. Many criticized this new idea and called it 'radical feminism', but by 1920 the U.S. congress passed a law giving women the right to vote.

Ella Wheeler Wilcox
"This is the 'new' religion; yet it is older than the universe. It is God's own thought put into practical form . . . . a religion which says: 'I am all goodness, love, truth, mercy, health. I am a necessary part of God's universe. I am a divine soul, and only good can come through me or to me." Ella Wheeler Wilcox. [2]

Andrew Jackson Davis
"His [Davis] chief work, *Nature's Divine Revelation*, was written in 1846", two years before the birth of U.S. spiritualism by the Fox Sisters. According to Abebooks.com this book was channeled from spirit to Davis while he was in a trance.

The birth of Spiritualism in the U.S.
The Fox Sisters (1848)
"Modern spiritualism -- the belief that it is possible to communicate with the spirits of the dead – started with the experiments of the Fox family in Hydesville, New York, after a disturbing series of taps and noises in their home." [3]

When the Fox sisters first heard rappings in their farmhouse, they set up a code in order to communicate with the spirit that was sending a message. The message was that he was a salesman and he had been buried in the cellar by someone who robbed and murdered him. Several years later a body was found there and next to him his case of wares.

There are several books about the Fox Sisters. Their experience in a Hydesville farmhouse created a great deal of attention, including some charlatans who made money on naïve individuals. One of the Fox sisters recanted after much harassment about the experience with spirit. But further reading indicates she wanted to end the harassment and so recanted under pressure. In any event, spiritualism took hold and there is a National Spiritualist Association of Churches. (See Appendix B for Declaration of Principles)

Lest one think the Fox Sisters did not start the spiritualism movement on a serious note, it might be interesting to see the names of some highly educated men who became converts to the movement:
Dr. Phelps, a Presbyterian minister in Stratford, CT, Prof. Hare of the University of PA, [state] Chief Justice Williams, Gov. Talmadge, General Bullard, Horace Greely, Fennimore Cooper, and William Cullen Bryant. [4]

It is extremely interesting to the author that both women who began the Suffrage Movement (to gain voting rights for women) had a psychic experience.

Susan B. Anthony
"Mrs. Stanton wrote in her diary:
    In a few days we are expecting Miss Anthony to make us a visit. She has had a very remarkable dream. The physician ordered her from Philadelphia to Atlantic City for her health. While in the latter place, she had a very vivid dream one night. She thought she was being burnt alive in one of the hotels, and when she arose in the morning, told her niece what she had dreamed. 'We must pack at once and go back to Philadelphia,' she said. This was done, and the next day the hotel in which they had been, ten other hotels and miles of the boardwalk, were destroyed by fire." [5]

Elizabeth Cady Stanton

" . . . At Washington, at a time when Congress was
sitting . . . [Stanton] . . . was told the house [hotel] was
full. After some hesitation the clerk, observing her
distress, undertook, if she would wait half an hour, that
a room . . . should be got ready for her. . . She went to
bed early and slept soundly till she was awakened by the
sensation of a hand touching her face, and a voice
cried, with a piteous accent, 'Oh, Mother! Mother!' She
determined to go to sleep again, and succeeded. Again
she was awakened with the hand nervously stroking her
face and the blood-curdling cry, 'Oh, Mother! Mother!'
It was no use trying to sleep. . . As soon as she heard
the servants moving she rang the bell and the
chambermaid came in with a startled look. To her the
visitor related her experiences.
'Yes, marm,' said the chambermaid, 'I told them they
ought not to have put you in the room. He was only
carried out an hour before you came.'
'Who was carried out?' said the lady.
'Why, the young man who has been lying here for a
fortnight in delirium tremens and died. He was
stretching out his hands, feeling for something, and
crying in heartbreaking voice, 'Oh, Mother! Mother!' " [6]

Hudson Tuttle

[Tuttle] wrote many books on the subject of spiritualism "the most
notable of these being *The Arcana of Nature* and *The Arcana of
Spiritualism*. The former of these works contained some quite
remarkable scientific material, yet it was completed in 1853, in the
author's eighteenth year. . . . It was quoted by . . . Darwin (*The Descent of
Man*, p.178)"[7]

Although several books have been written about spiritualism and
psychism, no public library will offer any of them. The reason is that
they are not considered 'mainstream' – for the general public.
It is such a misfortune for honest, dedicated spiritual seekers.

The advantage for such seekers is that used book stores who carry these books usually place a very low price on them all, making for inexpensive source material.

Sojourner Truth (1797-1883)
This evangelist and reformer, who was born a slave, became famous through her abolitionist efforts and public speeches. She often began her speech with this phrase: "Children, I speak to God and God speaks to me". This clearly described her conviction that she was a speaker inspired by God.

Robert Schumann (1810-1856)
"I must tell you a presentiment I have had; it haunted me from the 24th to the 27th of March, during which I was absorbed in my new compositions.

"There was a certain passage which obsessed me, and someone seemed to be repeating to me from the depths of his heart: *Ach Gott* (O, my God!) While composing I visualized funeral things, coffins, sorrowing faces. . . When I had finished, I sought for a title. The only which came to my mind was *Leichenphantasie* (Funeral Fantasy) . . . I was so overcome that the tears came to my eyes; I truly did not know why; . . . Then came Therese's letter, and all was clear. Her . . . sister in law's brother had just died."

"Schumann gave the title *Nachtstucke* (Nocturne) to that suite." [8]

Some methods of fortune telling, or prophecy, gained more and more popularity. Others had a short-lived existence such as phrenology. Phrenology – the study of bumps on the head – was popular in the mid-19th century and accepted by Henry Ward Beecher, Walt Whitman, and Clara Barton.

The Native American tribe of Paiute had their very own method of prophecy, known as the Ghost Dance.

Ghost Dance
"The prophetic founder of what has become known as the Ghost Dance of 1890 was a Paiute, Wovoka, who lived all his life in the Mason Valley of western Nevada . . .

"The ghost dance involved large numbers of people moving around a central tree. One characteristic feature was a trance many of the dancers experienced in which they visited the spirit world, conversed with dead relatives, and often caught glimpses of villages of native Americans living in the old way." [9]

Rebecca Ruter Springer
From her book, *Intra Muros*, published in 1890, Rebecca speaks of her experience 'on the other side,' which she visited while in a three –year coma:

> "Then the Savior began to speak, and the sweetness of his voice was far beyond the melody of the heavenly choir. And his gracious words! Would that I could, would that I dared, transcribe them as they fell from his lips. Earth has no language by which I could convey their lofty meaning. He first touched lightly upon the earth-life, and showed so wonderfully the link of light uniting the two lives – the past with the present. Then he unfolded to us some of the earlier mysteries of the blessed life, and pointed out the joyous duties just before us.

> "When he ceased, we sat with bowed heads as he withdrew. Our hearts were so enfolded, our souls so uplifted, our spirits so exalted, our whole being so permeated with his divinity, that when we arose we left the place silently and reverently, each bearing away a heart filled with higher, more divine aspirations, and clearer views of the blessed life upon which we were permitted to enter." [10]

Author's note: *Intra muros* was republished in 1994 with the title *Into the Light*.

Madame Blavatsky (1886)
Helena P. Blavatsky, author (*The Secret Doctrine*), a Russian prophet, "insisted [her prophecies] were not so much prophecies as positive knowledge, taught her by the Mahatmas of the East, Masters of Wisdom, possessors of an ancient knowledge which has never died out of the world, but which at times recedes into a necessary seclusion,

until it becomes once again imperative to broadcast it to the world . . . " [11]

America in prophecy

William Blake (1757-1827)
This mystical poet wrote a poem entitled *America: A Prophecy*. Although it is difficult to interpret the meaning "seems to be that the wisdom of the fathers, of Washington, Warren, Franklin, Paine, has made America unassailable; that, while flooded by materialism, it will not be too deeply submerged, and that diseases, repressions and errors cannot thrive on American soil". [12]

Andrew Jackson Davis (1845)
Davis "foresaw not only the ultimate spiritualization of America, but that this spiritualization would come about in virtue of leisure owing to numerous mechanical and labor-saving devices, many of which he foresaw with a quite remarkable lucidity." [13]

With all due respect to Mr. Davis, William Blake seems to be more on the mark, based on the following information provided by Archangel Gabriel in his seminar of August 10, 1991 entitled *Earth Changes, Earth Healing*. "That which is written upon your money will come to pass." He explained the symbolism on the back of the U.S. one dollar bill:

1. The pyramid symbolizes the female aspect "the sustaining power, that which has depth and substance".

2. The eye on top of the pyramid represents the masculine aspect "that which sees and acts upon".

"So you have here a balance . . . of the New Age, that is already cast into the ethers of your country: the action power and the sustaining power. Your government will find the people thereof, will wake up and realize that to fully be all that it can be, there has to be a perfect balance.

50

"The symbolism did not come by chance. It was given unto the men of that day to put upon your monies. . . it represents the destiny of your country. That destiny has not yet been fulfilled."

3. The triangle around the eye represents "the three aspects of man – body, mind, and spirit. . . on a higher level it represents the Father, Son, and Holy Ghost."

4. Annuit Coeptis. "It is written in a language that you do not read readily . . . 'The ideal of the New Age'."

5. Under the pyramid, the words MOVUS ORDO SECLORUM 'or New Order of the Century.'

CHAPTER 7
TWENTIETH CENTURY

"The Universe being wholly mental, it follows that it may be ruled only by Mentality. And in this truth is to be found an explanation of all the phenomena and manifestations of the various mental powers which are attracting so much attention and so much study in these earlier years of the Twentieth Century. . . . Mind must be the highest power affecting its [Universe] phenomena." [1]

Of course divination does not come to us through the physical form, but rather from our mental capacity to accept it. All humans have this capacity but most are unaware of it or fear it. We do not think with our brain. The brain *processes* thought. Ideas come from the mind. And our mind is part of the Divine Mind of God, our Creator. Some prophecies are terrifying, such as when one foresees war.

". . . early as 1905 . . . Madame de Thebes, the long-famous French clairvoyante, published these words in her annual "Almanac": . . . I see in the hands of distinguished Italians signs of a war of unprecedented violence. Germany threatens all of Europe in general and France in particular. . ." [2]

Other masters of divination prove by their own actions the power of the trained mind. From *Life and Teaching of the Masters of the Far East*, a member of an expedition to the Himalayas reports what he saw from the banks of a raging river:

> ". . . the twelve, fully dressed, walked to the bank of
> the stream, and with the utmost composure stepped on
> the water, not into it. I never shall forget my feelings as
> I saw each of those twelve men step from solid ground
> upon the running water . . . so astonished were we to
> see those twelve men walking calmly across the surface
> of the stream without the least inconvenience and not
> sinking below the soles of their sandals. When they
> stepped from the water to the farther bank I felt that
> tons of weight had been lifted off my shoulders, and I
> believe this was the feeling of every one of our party,

judging from the sighs of relief as the last man stepped ashore." [3]

At this time in history there have been several individuals who have demonstrated their ability to walk on hot coals. One of the members of the Himalayan expedition described walking through flames:

"The lightning ignited the grass . . . and before we knew it, we were virtually surrounded by a forest fire. . . [the guides] said 'There are two ways of escape. One is to try to get to the next creek, where there is water flowing through a deep canyon. . . about five miles away. . . the other way is to go on through the fire with us if you can trust us to take you through.'

. . .Throwing myself . . . wholly upon their protection, I stepped between them and we proceeded on our way, which seemed to be in the direction the fire was raging the most. Then immediately it seemed as if a great archway opened before us and we went on directly through that fire, without the least inconvenience, either from smoke or heat, . . there were at least six miles of this fire-swept area that we passed through. . . until we crossed a small stream and then were out of the fire" [4]

Gabriel explained to us the power of the mind and how little aware we are of it. He told a small group one day that if we all believed and focused we could light the city of Albany (where we sat at the time).

In the early 1900s, "Temple University founder Russell H. Conwell thought at first that his visions of his deceased wife, Sarah, were 'a delusion of age'. But the apparition, when it was tested, seemed to know things that he did not. Conwell said later that the implications of the case 'are of the deepest significance to religious thought'." [5]

When Jesus told his disciples that he would never leave us, he meant it quite literally. Through the centuries he has come with messages of promise and hope, of guidance and instructions on how to live – to those who accept him through spirit communication, for, after all, he

53

lives in the spirit world. Jesus spoke of the New Age, and from *The Logia* we quote: "These sayings are sent for the Elect Ones, His Servants. They are from the Faithful and True One, even Adonai. To-day they are restored that His Christs may understand who it is who speaketh again unto them; who they themselves were and are; what they once more were about to become; and the profound and vital part they are to take in the New Age and the restored true Drama of the Soul and the Planet." [6]

All nations, all languages and all religious leaders can – and often do — receive guidance from spirit.

"In 1935 a vision in the sacred lake of Lhamo Latso reportedly guided a Tibetan council to their new spiritual ruler; the fourteenth Dalai Lama was only two years old at the time." [7]

Rudolph Steiner (1861-1925)

Humans are endowed with imagination and when one dares to speak of divination and its benefits one is likely to hear that s/he merely has a vivid imagination. "When he was a boy . . . he became strangely aware of the presence of living beings who seemed invisible to the eyes of others. Some solitary children do develop an inner world of fantasy but Steiner's world seemed to have been one of direct perception rather than of imagination, for he was a realistic boy , gifted with an exact sense of order and a talent for mathematics." [8]

As an adult, Steiner "sees two forces perpetually at work in all evolution: the force that holds back . . . and a force *from outside the earth* that lifts the mind towards higher and higher consciousness and freedom . . ." [9]

Edgar Cayce (1877-1945)

Probably the greatest seer of the twentieth century [Cayce] is not listed in Biographical Names in the Eleventh edition of Merriam-Webster's Collegiate Dictionary. This only confirms the author's claim that 'modern man' still denies the possibility of communication between humans and spirit entities, thus ignoring all gifted people who have this talent. "The Cayce materials affirm over and again that there is indeed a far greater reality around us than what we dimly perceive through our limited sensory apparatus." [10]

The impact of Cayce's talent was widespread and affected people in all walks of life. "The 'sleeping' Edgar Cayce was . . . a psychic known to thousands of people, in all walks of life, who had cause to be grateful for his help. Indeed, many of them believed that he alone had either 'saved' or 'changed' their lives when all seemed lost. . . .[he] was a medical diagnostician, a prophet, and a devoted proponent of Bible lore." [11]

Cayce relates his first vision at age fourteen:
> "Kneeling by my bed that night, I prayed again that
> God would show me that He loved me, that He would
> give me the ability to do something for my fellow man
> which would show to them His love, even as the
> actions of His little creatures in the woods showed me
> their trust in one who loved them. . . .I was not yet
> asleep when the vision first began . . . A glorious light
> as of the rising morning sun seemed to fill the whole
> room, and a figure appeared at the foot of my bed. . . .
> an angel, or what, I knew not; but gently, patiently, it
> said, 'Thy prayers are heard. You will have you wish.
> Remain faithful. Be true to yourself. Help the sick, the
> afflicted." [12]

Cayce was a devout Christian and read the Bible often. Because of this, it was very unsettling for him to receive messages regarding reincarnation. But he had developed a great confidence in the source and came to accept the idea. His messages of healing were given to individuals, but he also received messages for humanity as a whole.

On channeling our Higher Self, how long should we wait to do i? How often must we remind ourselves of what St. Paul noted so long ago:
(For he saith, I have heard thee in a time accepted, and in the day of salvation have I succoured thee: behold, now is the accepted time; behold, now is the day of salvation). 11 Cor 6:2

"For with God nothing is impossible, and the individual that may give himself as a channel through which the influence of good may come to others may indeed be guided or shown the way.

For the influences of such a nature are those that all men seek, and for which there is a great cry in the earth today – and *today* IS the accepted time." [13]

We must always remember that throughout his life as a seer, Mr. Cayce was constantly beleaguered by those who ridiculed and questioned his work and his motives. In spite of all this, he continued to bring to humanity the wisdom we needed to hear.

> Here we are constantly impressed by the consuming
> dedication which drove this man through four decades
> of continual effort in attempting to aid and assist
> others. Why else would a man endure putting himself in
> an unconscious state some fifteen thousand times
> during a span of forty years, when on awakening he had
> no conscious recall of anything he ever said while
> asleep? Add to this his refusal to accept monetary
> returns beyond what was necessary for his modest
> immediate family needs – plus having to endure a non-
> ending stream of investigators and abuse from various
> sources – and we see a man who certainly had attained
> a firm inner belief in what he was doing. And if Cayce's
> life does not rank as a well-stated example of the
> Christian ethic, then how else can it be appraised? [14]

Edgar Cayce's Story of Jesus
Since our minds are part of the Mind of God, it is that Mind which is the source of all knowledge, and we have access to any knowledge we desire, at any time. We need only trust it is so, and listen.

"As the readings explained it, the knowledge gained while Cayce was in a self-induced sleep came principally from the subjects *own* unconscious mind. He was, in effect, simply "tuning in" to the correct frequency." [15]

This 'tuning in' can be done by all humans. And it is a talent that we all must learn in the days ahead, for we are much more than we know, as Gabriel explained.

Cayce's gift attracted much attention, some of it negative. "On several occasions he (Cayce) was jailed as a fraud, accused of cheap showmanship or of practicing medicine without a license. None of these claims were valid; he was a quiet, humble man who supported a wife and children more on faith than money." [16]

Now, at last, people dare to speak publicly of divination and TV has run several shows based on it.

"We've come a long way in the past few decades. We've now reached the point where individuals are publicly discussing ESP and psychic phenomena and asking questions about the subject." [17]

Cayce's readings and health messages were received while he was in a full trance state, meaning that he was unaware of what he was saying at the time. His messages were of a technical nature far beyond any comprehension of Cayce in a waking state. His readings were not even limited to English. From *Edgar Cayce on ESP* (p.65): "It has been estimated that during his lifetime Edgar Cayce spoke in some two dozen different languages while giving readings, although he had conscious knowledge only of English."

The extents of Cayce's readings increased over time.
"What followed were many years of helping people while in a self-induced state of unconsciousness, during which time Edgar had access to information on virtually any subject imaginable. . . At first the readings were limited to medical problems. Later, as the scope of his psychic ability expanded, such topics as meditation, dreams, reincarnation, and prophecy were included." [18]

Among the thousands of readings given by Cayce, some contained instructions on how to live our life on Earth. He often referred to Scripture, as he was learned in the Good Book: "If the experience is used for self-indulgence, self-aggrandizement, or self-exaltation, the entity does so to its own undoing, and creates for itself that which has been called karma and which must be met. And in meeting every error, every trial, every temptation, whether they be mental or physical experiences, the approach to it should always be in the attitude of: 'Not my will, but Thine, O God, be done in and though me'." [19]

Edgar Cayce was a devout Christian, loved the Bible, before *and after* his experiences with spirit communication. As he provided others with information about healing and prophecy, his devotion to Scripture deepened. "Quite early in life I became a student of the Scriptures, and love them yet. It seems to me the Scriptures tell us about every phase of psychic power." [20]

Much has been presented here about Edgar Cayce because of his 15,000 healing messages and many books have been written to pass on his lessons for humanity. We are truly blessed to have messages from spirit through many individuals through the past 150 years. One such spiritual teacher was St.Germain, an ascended master, who visited a small group of seekers in the 1930s, in the U.S.

Saint Germain (1932)

"The thirty-three Discourses contained in this book (*The "I AM" discourses*) were dictated over a *visible* Light and Sound Ray in our home during 1932, by the Ascended Master Saint Germain and those other Ascended Masters directly concerned with this Activity. The sound of His Voice was physically audible to everyone in the room. At times His Visible, Tangible Presence also stood within the room — when He radiated the Power and Energy of the Light Rays to accomplish special work." [21]

Johannes Greber (1932)

The last person anyone would expect to embrace spirit communication is a Roman Catholic priest, yet in the 19th century a priest in Germany had an experience which turned his attention to it, and he wrote a book about his experiences. Greber came to believe in, then communicate with, the spirit world. He wrote of his spiritual path in *Communication with the Spirit World of God*. He recognized the impact which spiritism had on Scripture. He says, in his Introduction, page 3:

"In this battle against spiritism, the churches are fighting in the front rank . . . Judaism and Christianity are based upon the testimony of the Old and New Testaments and hence rest entirely upon spiritism, for of all spiritist works the greatest is the Bible, the larger part of whose contents hinges upon messages sent from the Beyond."

The tragedy of our ignorance about spirit communication is that the spirit world is full of angels and ascended masters who long to bring wisdom from on high to our consciousness. In the 1930s, in the mountains of Colorado, a group met in an obscure cave to listen to an ascended master, Saint Germain. His teachings were written down and published in several volumes. I was fortunate enough to find two of the volumes in used bookstores. One is entitled *The "I AM" Discourses* and the other one is entitled *The Magic Presence*.

From the *Tribute* of *The Magic Presence Vol II* (p.vi), Godfre Ray King states:

"The hour is at hand when the humanity of this Earth must give more recognition to the Activity of the Great Ascended Masters and Angelic Host, who are constantly pouring out Their Transcendent Light and Assistance to mankind. There must come more conscious cooperation between the outer physical life of humanity and these Great Beings who are the Protectors and Teachers of the human beings in this World."

Divination finally came into its own in America, then spread around the world, in the 1960s. The huge popularity of Von Daniken's book, *Chariots of the Gods?* proved that humanity is hungry for such information.

Erich Von Daniken (1968)
[In France, in the 1960s] "Books on astrology, reincarnation, and visitors from outer space rolled off the presses, and there was no sign of any loss of interest. The craze spread to other countries, notably Germany, England, and the United States. In 1968 a German book called *Remembrance of the Future* made a fortune and a name for its author, Erich von Daniken. Translated into English as *Chariots of the Gods?* It sold more copies [that year] than any other book except the Bible." [22]

Arthur Ford (1971)
"Arthur Ford was one of the best-known trance mediums of this century. He was the man who communicated the great Houdini's last

59

message to the world [from spirit]; he was the medium through whom Bishop Pike spoke to his dead son; it is his spirit that has introduced Ruth Montgomery to A WORLD BEYOND.

"But Arthur Ford was more than a man who made headlines. . . In this book (*The Life Beyond Death*), written shortly before his own death, is the evidence that Arthur Ford collected through research and personal experience to show that life beyond death exists." [23]

We tend to deny spirit communication as a spurious method used by New Agers, yet spirit entities constantly bring messages to all who are willing to listen. The Roman Catholic Church decreed the end of revelation, according to Borgia: "The Earth has never been left high and dry, without someone to tell them about all this [spirit world]. Lately, the flow of revelation has increased, but you must remember that one of the greatest ecclesiastical establishments on earth has long ago decreed that all revelation ceased when the last of the apostles passed from the earth . . . " [24]

If people dare to question the above paragraph, they are judging the Bible. Fundamentalists see this as anathema. And yet, without acceptance of spirit communication we are doomed to suffer the consequences, for spirit will guide us through any and all problems we encounter on Earth, including earthquakes and tidal waves.

All prophecy is not exact, but it is interesting to compare the predictions of clairvoyants and astrologers regarding WWI:

". . . virtually all astrologers predicted a terrible conflict for Europe and notably for Germany between the years 1913 and 1916. Clairvoyants, on the other hand, more frequently specified the years 1913-1915 as a period boding disastrous days for Germany and Austria as the result of a world war." [25]

It is rare to find a scientist who accepts divination. In 1940 it was even more rare. In 1940, Mr. Forman wrote: "In these scientific modern times . . . virtually no one believes in prophecy . . . Yet an eminent biologist like Dr. Alexis Carrel, among the foremost in the world, . . . quite simply informs us that he has been interested in the phenomena

60

of telepathy and clairvoyance in the same manner that he has been interested in physiology, chemistry and pathology; and that both telepathy and clairvoyance are a normal, although rare, activity of the human being." [26]

Now, 72 years later, these phenomena are publicly spoken of, with impunity.

Anthony Borgia, (1958)
"To discover what kind of place is the next world, we must inquire of someone who lives there, and record what is said. That is what has been done in this present volume.
"The communicator, whom I first came to know in 1909 – five years before his passing into the spirit world – was known on earth as Monsignor Robert Hugh Benson, a son of Edward White Benson, former Archbishop of Canterbury. . . . it has been my privilege to act as his recorder." [27]

Two books were thus transcribed from the spirit world. *Beyond This Life* Borgia gives "an account of his passing and his subsequent travels through various parts of spirit lands. . . . in *The World Unseen* Borgia "deals at much greater length with a number of important and interesting facts and facets of spirit life." [28]

Some of the topics listed in the Contents of *The World Unseen* are Halls of Learning, Music, Recreations, The Children's Sphere, and Occupations. Borgia closes the book as follows: "To give you a comprehensive account of all that we have seen in the world of spirit would fill many volumes, and therefore I have chosen what I felt would be of most interest and benefit. . . ." [29]

Much has been written about messages from the unseen world of spirit, and many messages have been put in print. Some experiences in/with the 'other side' cannot be put into words; the plethora of information available precludes writing them all.

Kathleen McConnell (1971)
An example of Earth-bound children. Mrs. McConnell had no prior experience with spirit communication. But upon discovering that three small spirit children resided in her attic, she named them and learned to

61

communicate with them. "In 1971 Kathleen McConnell and her family moved into a historic home known as the Fontaine Manse. Two days after moving in, she and her husband had an extraordinary experience that left them with no doubt that unseen residents occupied the house, too. . . spirit children who lived in the attic of the mansion – Angel Girl, Buddy, and The Baby." [30]

After writing several chapters about the 'other children' living in her attic, Kathleen finally sees them return to Heaven. She describes the event as follows: "The dull, dismal attic was filled with a brilliant light that did not come from the sunshine . . . I knew choirs of angels were singing to welcome my babies home. I was finished and so were they . . . I was content that I hadn't given these children up. I had given them back." [31]

Judy Boss (1972)
In her book *In Silence They Return*, Judy opens the Introduction as follows:
"Death is not really the end," I said to my neighbor shortly after my husband was killed, leaving me with five small children to raise alone. "For him, it is an exciting new adventure." And for me life is a challenge that I have to face. I have no time for tears."

After receiving a message from her husband, then in spirit, Mrs. Boss said to his heard but unseen self, "Thank you, Mac, Not only have you given me a meaningful philosophy for our children to be raised with, but you have left me with proof of your existence." [32]

Psychic Healers (1985)
Holistic medicine is beginning to receive some acceptance. In the future it will be the only kind of medical treatment, as doctors see the patient from a psychological and mental viewpoint, rather than from merely a symptom to be treated. Doctors and patients will learn to use their intuition regarding maintenance of their health.

". . . the laws of health are little understood even today, particularly the effect of spiritual factors on health . . .We are only beginning to be aware of the intuitional forces." [33]

Native American Prophecy
In 1931, when Black Elk was a young boy, he had a vision. When he was only nine he "fell ill and lay near death for twelve days". As an aged man, he told about the vision to poet John G. Neihardt: "Two spirits came down from the sky . . . and with them Black Elk ascended to 'a world of cloud' . . . Black Elk met the six Grandfathers, the most powerful spirits of the world . . . The Grandfathers taught Black Elk about the spiritual values of life and presented him with symbols of their powers . . .Black Elk was dismissed by the oldest Grandfather, who told him, 'Go back with power to the place from whence you came.' His illness was cured. But he had changed forever." [34]

Native American physical phenomena: According to the Lakota, the *heyoka* are those who have seen the Thunderbird in a vision, and because of this they are able to reach into boiling water with bare hands to take out pieces of boiled dog meat during the *heyoka* ceremony; they are able to predict stormy weather, and in some cases to control it. Whenever we 'channel' information from an unseen source, it is important to know that the unseen source has a name. Its name is the akashic records.

Akashic Records defined
1. "Shirley [MacLaine] reacted skeptically. ' On what do you base that information?' she asked. The voice then gave Shirley a lesson in metaphysics. He described the *Akashic Records* as an invisible dimension, a Hall of Records, where *all* thoughts and experiences are stored. All information there can be contacted psychically." [35]

In fact, it is the akashic records which are 'read' by an efficient medium. Another definition:

2. " They might be said to represent the memory of the universe, but that would still be rather vague. The word *akasha* is a Sanskrit term referring to one of the constituents of the natural world, the other ones being earth, water, fire and air. According to ancient tradition, it is an infinitely subtle substance, a form of energy in which the universe bathes, and which is capable of storing the visual and auditive memory of all life." [36]

63

Past Life Regression

Understanding the akashic records, one can comprehend how past life regressions occur. My personal experience with past life regression follows. At no time was I hypnotized. Only one time I was in another level of consciousness (see #8 following, 500 A.D.)

1. At the second reading by Millie Coutant (see Preface), to my great amazement, the first thing she saw was myself as a schoolteacher, picking up exactly where she had left off at the conclusion of the first reading! She described me and my clothing: I looked about the same as I do now, but hair pulled back in a bun, wearing a long dress. She never gave dates, but said it was when we were 'moving west'. Probably it was the nineteenth century. After a time I took a boat down the Mississippi to meet my sister who lived in the south. There I met a man and married.

She continued to describe other past lives:
2. In the early years of America (probably eighteenth century), I came here, at the age of two, with my parents. My father was a missionary. I was climbing on the railing and my mother told me to get down. The trip had been a very stormy one. Millie saw my father talking to the captain, on the deck, as we headed to this country. When asked by my father when we would arrive, the captain said, "In a thrice". Millie turned to me and said, "What is a 'thrice'?" I told her, but was astonished that she could 'see' my past incarnation and alternately talk to me. Never since have I seen this done. One of the greeters said, "We have a place for ye to stay". Millie asked why they talked so funny. I explained that was how they spoke in those days. The details provided by Millie were unbelievable. She saw us dock on an island in Boston Harbor, greeted by many. She saw men moving our trunks into the house, and up the stairs. She saw a cat running down the stairs, a pot under my bed, and books on a small table by the bed.

Millie then saw me as a teenager, writing down my father's sermons as he spoke them, all the while pacing back and forth. (in later years I realized he was channeling his sermon from spirit, but asked me to write it down. I still wonder why he didn't channel as he spoke from the lectern – as an inspirational speaker). I think I admired him and his ability to 'get' a sermon as he did. In this lifetime these ambitions were realized.

3. I lived in France, near Paris, with my maternal grandmother and an aunt, because my mother had died. I believe this was in the 17th century. Millie described a scene in which I was sitting with my grandmother in front of a fireplace. I was very young. She called me her 'little bitty'. Suddenly my father arrived in a horse and buggy, demanding that he take me immediately to Paris to live with his mother. Distraught, my grandmother helped me pack to leave. My paternal grandmother was wealthy, provided me with fine clothing and a prosperous life. I married a man who later was kicked by a horse and died. I returned to my childhood home and learned that my grandmother had passed. I took my aunt back to Paris to live with me.

4. Based on Millie's description of another life, I would place it around the fifteenth century. I was married to a tavern owner in Ireland. I was scrubbing the floor since men were spitting all over (apparently before spittoons). I was cursing men because of the filthy floor and because of a war that was then being fought. We had two children, possibly six and eight years of age. I was lying in bed with terrible pain. My two children stood in the doorway, looking at me and wondering what was wrong. My husband came in and said, "Are you that way again?" And I said, "No, this is different". A doctor was called, but Millie said he didn't know anything about medicine. Millie said I died shortly after that, from a burst appendix.

5. Then, going way back, Millie described another life, in either Rome or Greece. When I was a young woman I told my parents I wanted to 'travel the world', which they said I could not do without a chaperone. I told them I had one. So I went.

Millie saw me, later in that incarnation, going into a huge hall to listen to a speaker. Women were not allowed there, but I knew some young men and they got me into the back of the auditorium. Later, Millie saw me married to a 'maker of laws'. We were wealthy. We had no children. Then Millie saw my husband getting out of a carriage in front of a large building. As he walked up the steps, he was stabbed by an 'enemy'. He collapsed and died. Then Millie saw me sitting by a window, alone and grieving, and I died.

Because of the detailed descriptions, and knowing that Millie was highly regarded as a medium, I fully accepted the readings as valid. All her readings were recorded and I occasionally listen to them again. Later I learned that her ability to see spirit is called clairvoyance and her ability to hear spirit clairaudience. I received many messages from spirit in later years.

6. In a short reading one day a medium told me that I was a young man and had been killed by a snake that wrapped itself around me and suffocated me. Neither the year or the country was provided. I still fear snakes.

7. I was a Native American Indian chief (male), and one of my current daughters was my daughter then. She was 'greatly loved and admired'.

8. It was about the year 500 A.D. I was a man in that lifetime. I must have been a teacher or minister, as I was passing on the teachings of Jesus Christ. I was married but had no children. When I was about thirty I was killed for heresy.

9. Archangel Gabriel described another past life. He did not give personal messages as a rule because he told us there are mediums and psychics who can answer our questions. He came to tell us about ourselves, our Source and our journey back home to God. (whom we never left, except in our consciousness.). One evening, at a question and answer session of about fifteen people, he explained that in this lifetime we are learning lessons from our errors of a past life. One woman went to the microphone and asked what past life she was dealing with now. Gabriel said "If I tell you, everyone else will want to know." And everyone called out, "Yes, tell us." Gabriel told the man recording to turn off the microphone. We all understood why: he was about to tell each of us a personal history that others need not know.

In hindsight, I wish I had not asked. But this is what he told me when it was my turn to hear him: I was a queen and was known as 'Bloody Mary'. I was also called 'queen of the guillotine'." When he said 'Bloody Mary' I cringed, because as an active alcoholic for several years, this was one of my favorite drinks.

In this lifetime, history has never interested me much, so I had to look it up. I was Mary I, Mary Tudor, queen of England, 1553-1558. Then one day I asked my son Roy what he knew about Bloody Mary, Queen of England. He said, "Well, she had 167 people killed by the guillotine or burned at the stake, why?" I said, "I just wondered." Somehow I could not bring myself to tell him. Probably because it was such a shameful lifetime and also because I believed that he did not accept the idea of reincarnation.

I do not write about these lifetimes to convince you that reincarnation is true, but rather to explain how spirit communication works - that some mediums are capable of reading the Akashic Records and telling us what they 'see' there.

And so the mystery of someone reading past lives is solved, for there in the ethers is the recorded history of all humanity, available to those who can tap into it psychically. Besides this reading of the Akashic Records, communication exists between earthlings and spirit entities because there is merely a thin veil between the two which, unfortunately, is seen by us as a thick, impenetrable wall. Now is the time to wake up to this wonderful tool of communication. Now is the time to KNOW that God sends his messengers constantly to help us learn about ourselves. And to learn about how we can go back home to stay and get off this karmic ride that brings us back time and again to Earth for yet another lesson. Gabriel told us that we have lived so many lifetimes on Earth that we have met everyone now on the planet. This is a staggering fact.

CHAPTER 8
AN ARCHANGEL VISITS EARTH

Archangel Gabriel came to a small group of spiritual seekers in Albany, New York. This author listened to Archangel Gabriel (1987-1999)– with many others – wide awake and fully aware of the full trance channeling taking place. Gabriel was consistently loving and truthful. He took questions about his teachings and all were welcome to attend. A significant fact that he imparted to us was that eleven others – ascended masters – came to various parts of the Earth at the same time Gabriel did; all with the same lesson he brought: Wake up, humans, you are all children of God, and must learn to live from the Lord God of Your Being.

The reader might ask how these 12 locations were chosen to receive guidance from the spirit world. Obviously, they had to be centers of light in which such communication was accepted. This proves that there are many places on Earth where communication with the spirit world is accepted, and that spirit entities are aware of those locations and are drawn to them to help awaken all humanity. These centers will spread the word of the New Age of Truth and pass on the teachings to those willing to listen.

With the acceptance that angels can communicate with us, how much more holy, how much more gratifying, how much more wondrous is it that an archangel (Gabriel) came to inform us for a span of twelve years – not only teaching us, but willingly answering all questions put to him. He is the Announcer of the Ages, and came to announce the Age of Aquarius. He said it is also the truth age. What an exciting era to live in! How blessed I was to be in that sacred space in which he taught! Archangel Gabriel visited Earth many times, from 1987 to 1999, by channeling through Rev. Penny A. Donovan, a dedicated medium and ordained Bishop. Some of Gabriel's teachings can be found in *Getting to Know Your Soul*, which was compiled by Rev. Penny Donovan and Mary I. Lee-Civalier, and published in 2004. The dedication reads:

"To all who on their spiritual journey dare to listen, question, and take on the challenges that cause them to learn, grow, and love more than they ever thought possible. Their dedication to their spiritual growth gives rise to and reason for this book."

Future generations will have the benefit of Gabriel's teachings, as all his copyrighted lessons were faithfully recorded and made available. See www.sacredgardenfellowship.org

Regarding our self-awareness Gabriel said, "In becoming aware of yourselves as spiritual beings, you become aware of life in a slightly different manner. When you are aware of your spiritual selves, you touch into the truth of your being. You become aware that there *is* a truth of your being that should be ardently sought after and brought out into a living-ness in your experiences." [1]

At this time we have Gabriel's word that we have many 'bodies' – physical, emotional (astral), mental and spiritual. The spirit self of us never leaves us, for it is eternal. We are simply unaware of it. When we cross over from earthly life to heavenly life, we shed the out-worn physical body and live on the astral plane in our astral body. Yet the spirit, soul and personality – as well as our memory – continue on the astral plane.

Archangel Gabriel told us that he brought no new information, but simply reminded us what we already know, but have forgotten. He made it clear to us that there is no 'hell' with 'eternal fires' of punishment to which anyone ever goes after so-called 'death'. Nor is there an entity anywhere that is known as the devil. What Mr. Swedenborg (18th Century) describes as hell is a desolate kind of place to which humans go who *expect to find such a place on the other side*. It is the lower astral plane. Most humans go to the higher astral plane, where perfect love, joy, and constant light prevail. As in our earthly life, what we expect is what we receive, and how we live our lives on Earth will set the stage for our entry into Heaven when we transition.

Scripture omits several years of Jesus' life, for reasons unknown. From the age of twelve, when he was found in the Temple, until his appearance at the Jordan River to be baptized by John, we have no information about the Master's whereabouts or activities. In the twentieth century we were blessed to find a book entitled *The Aquarian Gospel of Jesus the Christ,* which was given to Levi by spirit early in the 20th century. Gabriel confirmed its authenticity. It describes Jesus' journey throughout the known world. At a feast In Persia, he was asked about the devil and hell-fires. His answer was:

"Whatever God, the One, has made is good, and like the great First Cause, the seven spirits all are good, and everything that comes from their creative hands is good.

"Now, all created things have colours, tones and forms their own; but certain tones, though good and pure themselves, when mixed, produce inharmonies, discordant tones.

"And certain things, though good and pure, when mixed, produce discordant things, yea, poisonous things, that men call evil things.

"So evil is the inharmonious blending of the colours, tones, or forms of good.

"Now, man is not all-wise, and yet has will his own. He has the power, and he uses it, to mix God's things in a multitude of ways, and every day he makes discordant sounds, and evil things.

"And every tone and form, be it of good, or ill, becomes a living thing, a demon, sprite, or spirit of a good or vicious kind.

"Man makes his devil thus; and then becomes afraid of him and flees; his devil is emboldened, follows him away and casts him into torturing fires.

"The devil and the burning fires are both the works of man, and none can put the fires out and dissipate the evil one, but man who made them both." [2]

There is some hesitation to paraphrase or recap any message which Gabriel gave us. However, reporting in full a six hour seminar is prohibitive and illegal. I will do my best to convey the essence of the day's lesson.

At Lily Dale on August 10, 1991 Gabriel gave an all day seminar on *Earth Changes, Earth Healing*, in which he described the changes in the topography of Earth after the Earth changes, which are coming in 2012. It will definitely NOT be the end of the world; only the end of the world *as we know it*. Preparation should be made, but hoarding should not be done. He told us the reason for the upheaval is that humanity has polluted the air, soil, and water to such an extent that Mother Earth will shake in order to cleanse herself. Humanity has progressed in technology at the expense of spiritual growth. We must start anew, so to speak, to see if we can get it right this time. The U.S. was intended to be an example for humankind on how to live in a state of peace and brotherhood. Obviously we have gone far astray. Now we will have another opportunity to fulfill this plan.

I recalled this information from Gabriel when I read Madame Blavatsky's prediction of a new humanity: "Thus it is the mankind of the New World . . .whose mission and Karma it is to sow the seeds for a forthcoming, grander, and far more glorious Race than any of those we know of at present. The cycles of Matter will be succeeded by cycles of spirituality and a fully developed mind." [3]

Jesus, Mary and many others, such as Pilate, were all members of the Essene community, according to Gabriel.

Meurois-Givaudan, A.and Meurois-Givaudan, D. (1992)
"The following account [fruit of a patient reading of the Akashic Records] takes the readers back some two thousand years to ancient Palestine, into the heart of the Essene community. . . .the readers are offered a firsthand vision of the personality and teachings of Jesus, his life and the lives of the disciples." [4]

Jesus Speaks to us in Every Age

Jesus the Christ speaks to the Essenes

> "I need some time to be alone, to compare the path I
> have taken with the one that still lies ahead of me. A
> father does not make of his son a device to carry out
> his plans. Therefore, in giving me a man's body, my
> celestial Father gave me a man's freedom as well. This
> is a sign of love that you must understand. The two
> hands of the human creature, the choice open to him in
> the making of his life here on Earth are the first fruits
> of his oncoming grandeur, more than you can imagine.
> Strip these ideas of the words that cover them. I show
> you a pathway for humanity. Looking at the times that
> are to come, I fear one thing: that which is not
> understood gives rise to terror, fanaticism, or a
> withering devotion. So I tell you, do not make a god of
> me." [5]

The Author

The author had a glorious experience in March of 1984, during my first
séance. Shortly after the circle commenced, I saw the Master standing
about 8 feet in front of me. His brilliant blue eyes held my gaze. His
hair was auburn with reddish highlights. His arms were outstretched
toward me and on his upturned hands was a huge loaf of bread. He
said to me, "Lay down your life for me, and I will give you the bread of
life". I did not understand his words at that time, but as the ensuing
weeks unfolded I stopped my addiction to alcohol. Then it became
clear to me that if I surrendered to his guidance I could be blessed by
him with a lasting sobriety. And I know now that Jesus *always* keeps his
promise.

The Christ (1986)

Virginia Essene and 45 other 'meditators' traveled to Israel in 1984.
Virginia was a college professor until she was guided "under the
direction of my soul's intention" to write. One of her books, *New
Teachings for an Awakening Humanity*, was written 'to help us remember
why we came to earth', and was given to her by Christ Jesus. From
Jesus the Christ himself, through "Virginia", in 1986:

"This is my own statement sent directly to you, not mere reports of my sayings and actions recorded later by the disciples . . . My words are not intended just for so-called Christians but for everyone.
These words address the immediate conditions that your earthly negativity has caused and which must change if you are to prevent serious repercussions. They are serious because I love you and would call your attention to the emergency state in which you reside." [6]

The Master Jesus Recorded (1997-1998)
Of the many seminars presented by Archangel Gabriel, three were devoted to the Master Jesus, as follows:

Master Jesus
 On Jan. 18, 1997 Gabriel described some of the most important past lifetimes Jesus spent on Earth, including Melchizedek, Joseph (coat of Many Colors), and Buddha. Scripture mentions Melchizedek. Joseph was the first human being to demonstrate forgiveness. Buddha believed that wisdom was the most important attribute of man. Upon his transition he realized the most important attribute is love. After 500 years of surrendering totally to the Will of God, he manifested as Jesus and became the Christ.

Master Jesus II
In the seminar of May 17, 1997, Gabriel describes the Essene community and its rites, rules and regulations. Mary, Joseph and Jesus were all members. Gabriel also told of many things that occurred but are not found in scripture. He suggested that we study the Dead Sea Scrolls. He told us of Jesus' relationships with his apostles, before and after the crucifixion. He explained that Jesus came not to be worshipped, but followed. It is clearly stated in the Bible that he came as a way-shower, an example. He often said, 'follow me.'

Master Jesus III
Jesus came to clarify some of his own words in the Bible. This seminar was presented on January 17, 1998. Jesus expounded on the Sermon on the Mount and his other teachings of 2,000 years ago. Also, he verified his authorship of *A Course in Miracles*.

Porter and Lippmann (1986)

In 1985 Grady Porter and Glenda Lippmann wrote an Introduction to their book *Conversations with JC,* explaining -

> "We continued meditating regularly for about two
> months. It was very peaceful and relaxing
> . . . Then one day, Grady had a breakthrough. In
> meditation, she saw herself leaning against this big rock,
> high on a mountaintop. It was a beautiful setting, and
> she could see forever in all directions. Then, the
> perspective changed and she was *in* the picture. She was
> now leaning on the rock and actually looking out at the
> view. She described it this way: 'As I looked about at
> the beauty, I became aware of a figure coming toward
> me. He looked vaguely familiar, dressed in his long
> white robe. He had beautiful auburn hair, and a rich
> reddish beard. But it was his smile, his dancing, glowing
> eyes, his radiating joy, that just took my breath away
> . . .You're Jesus? I asked'. He just smiled bigger and
> again, just nodded his head up and down." [7]

CHAPTER 9
TWENTY-FIRST CENTURY

John Edwards (1999-2004)
John received a reading from a medium when he was young. Of that
reading, he shared the following in an interview: "She told me I would
one day become internationally known for my psychic abilities through
lectures, books, radio and TV. I thought she was full of it until she
started to tell me things no one in my life knew about . . . The details
were unbelievable." [1]

Of course her prophecy came true, as we all know. "Edward was the
producer and host of the show *Crossing Over with John Edward . . .*
broadcast on SCI FI Channel in the United States and on LIVINGtv in
the UK . . .he gave [psychic] readings to audience members." [2]

Mia Dolan (2003)
Mia Dolan is now one of England's best known psychics.
"She was twenty-two when she first heard a voice she could not
explain. She had always considered herself to be a down-to-earth
person and certainly never believed in psychic phenomena . . . Finally,
Mia discovered that she had a rare psychic gift and learned how to
control and use it." [3]

U.S. Government and divination
Irrelevancy of Time and Space in Telepathy: "Thirty-five years after
our initial experiments Astronaut Edgar D. Mitchell, during the Apollo
14 flight, January 31 to February 9th, 1971, with the aid of four selected
sensitives, of whom I was not one, conducted a series of telepathic
experiments, which were judged significant, from moon to earth, in the
neighborhood of 150,000 miles, proving once again that time and
space are no barrier to the mind." [4]

Visions of the Deceasd
When survivors have a vision of loved ones after death it must indicate
that they accept the *idea* of life after death. A friend of mine used to
say, "Everyone attends their own funeral". She meant as a spirit, from
the 'other side'.

"The universal experience of apparitions has found its way into the language and folklore of cultures all over the world, from a time long before the beginning of recorded history. . . . A number of studies published in medical journals and other scholarly sources have established that a high percentage of bereaved persons have visions of the deceased . . . as many as 66% of widows experience apparitions of their departed husbands." [5]

Sometimes those in spirit choose to reveal themselves in a photo taken after their death. Mary Todd Lincoln, as a widow, appeared for a formal photo incognito (veiled in mourning). When the print was taken, the photographer recognized an apparition standing behind Mrs. Lincoln as the late president. "Mary Lincoln agreed, and added, 'I am his widow'." [6]

Angelic help for earthlings

Angels, Gabriel told us, attend every meeting of world leaders and do their best to influence them in positive directions. But, of course, all humans have free choice which angels cannot override.

There is some conjecture as to whether Abraham Lincoln received instructions to free the slave population. Perhaps he did.

"It remains a subject of argument between historians and Spiritualists as to the extent to which Lincoln was influenced by spirit guidance in his decision to free the slaves. Certainly at the start of the Civil War it had not been his intention to end slavery in the South." [7]
Powerful leaders in history have consulted mediums. Several occupants of the U.S. White House have done so. Queen Victoria, ruler of England for over 60 years, found solace in knowing her husband was alive in spirit. Queen Victoria's personal manservant, John Brown, "reportedly was also a medium who enabled the widowed Queen to communicate with her beloved Albert. The evidence for Brown's mediumship is mixed, but the Queen certainly believed that he had genuine premonitions of the future, and relied on him greatly." [8]

John Brown was not the only medium who brought Queen Victoria comforting words from her deceased husband.

"According to his daughter, Eva Lee, Robert James Lee was only 13 or 14 when he delivered his first spirit message to Queen Victoria from Prince Albert. Miss Lee says the messages went on until the Queen's death." [9]

More recently, it is reported: UK's Princess Diana consulted New Age healers and spiritualists. Website of guardian.co.uk

Gabriel told us that Woodrow Wilson received the idea of League of Nations from spirit. Even more startling, Gabriel explained that FDR had also been advised by spirit. Pres. Roosevelt listened to some of it, but not all of the guidance. *If he had followed all of it there would not have been a second world war.* This hit me to the core, for I was a young teenager during WWII, and recalled too vividly the horror of it, the slaughter of it, and the unimaginable devastation of the atomic bomb. Casualties included the loss of my brother 1st Lt. Charles Blake Wallace, who gave his life in Europe.

Gabriel told us this fascinating story about WWII: The Germans were planning to attack England, from submarines in the English Channel. Word got out somehow and the mediums and psychics in England heard about it. All the men in their twenties and thirties were off to war, so the women gathered the young and the elderly. They were told to bring stovepipes, brooms and mops to the cliffs. All this innocuous material was arranged in such a way that as the moon shone on them at night, they looked like guns and cannons. When the Germans viewed this array through their periscopes, they sent word back that armaments were mounted to greet them. The attack was called off. Of course, if the attack had been planned in daylight there would have been a totally different outcome.

There is another story about WWII I would like to relate. It was told to me by a friend of mine who had the experience.

She was planning a vacation trip to Hawaii with her fiancé when her brother asked her if she was going to see the memorial at Pearl Harbor. She told him that she did not plan to go there. He pleaded with her, saying that he probably would never get there himself. So she agreed.

Although my friend had a fine psychic ability, she had no intention of using it on this vacation trip.

As she and her fiancé approached the site where the sunken warship could be seen, she heard a male voice speak his name and the name of another sailor. He gave their rank and said that they had gone down with the ship. But he also said (paraphrased), "We don't understand why everyone is so sad and come crying. We agreed to this experience and we are still very much alive here." My friend remembered the names, and as they left the memorial site she scanned the list of casualties. The two names were listed there!

Out of Body Experience

In 1978 Guideposts of Carmel, NY, published a 2-in-1 book including *My Glimpse of Eternity* by Betty Malz and *Return from Tomorrow* by G.G. Ritchie, Jr. and Elizabeth Sherrill. I quote here from each.

From *My Glimpse of Eternity:*
"It happened when she was twenty-seven years old. In the Union Hospital of Terre Haute, Indiana a 5 A..M. on a July morning, 1959, Betty was pronounced dead . . .". In *My Glimpse of Eternity* (Intro, p.12), Betty describes her experience on the other side of that dividing line that we call 'death,' then how she returned to her body on the hospital bed – to the stunned amazement of her grieving father and the hospital personnel.

"The transition was serene and peaceful. I was walking up a beautiful green hill . . . I was walking on grass, the most vivid shade of green I had ever seen . . . the texture of fine velvet; every blade was alive and moving . . . there was no darkness, no uncertainty, only a change in location and a total sense of well-being." [10]

After relating in detail her experience on 'the other side' with angels Betty wrote, "I was back in my hospital bed now and the letters stretched all the way from the window, past my bed and on into the room. They read: *I am the resurrection and the life; he that believeth in me, though he were dead, yet shall he live.*" [11]

From *Return from Tomorrow:*

> "I was pronounced dead – sheet pulled up over my
> head. The fact that after ten minutes or so I was
> brought back to live a while longer on this earth is to
> me just a parenthesis in a much bigger story. . . .
> Whatever I saw was only --- from the doorway, so to
> speak. But it was enough to convince me totally of two
> things from that moment on. One, that our
> consciousness does not cease with physical death – that
> it becomes in fact keener and more aware than ever.
> And secondly, that how we spend our time on earth,
> the kind of relationships we build, is vastly, infinitely
> more important than we can know." [12]

There are varying descriptions of 'the other side' from those who have
experienced a NDE, but the one constant seems to be the calm
peacefulness and acceptance, with no lingering doubts or fears from
the Earth plane.

The Transition Experience

Anthony Borgia, in his book entitled *Life in the World Unseen*, describes
the moment of passing into the spirit world at so-called 'death':

"I had a presentiment that my days on earth were drawing to a close
only a short while before my passing . . . Many times I had a feeling of
floating away and of gently returning . . . and yet I had the sensation of
the most extraordinary exhilaration of the mind. . . I had no fear, no
misgivings, no doubts, no regrets . . . All that I wanted was to be away.
"I suddenly felt a great urge to rise up . . .I found that I was actually
doing so . . . I then beheld what had taken place. I saw my physical
body lying lifeless upon its bed, but there was I, the *real* I, alive and
well." [13]

From Beyond the Grave

Arthur Ford

Shortly after the death of Arthur Ford, renowned psychic, his close friend Ruth Montgomery wrote:

"No sooner had I murmured my usual prayer for protection and placed my fingers in touch-typing position than the [automatic] writing began:

"Ruth, this is Lilly and the group. Arthur Ford is here and wants you to know that he is as young as the merry month of May. He feels great and does not want you to grieve. He is so glad to be here, more delighted than you will ever know . . ." [14]

Those who have transitioned to the next realm will find a way to contact us, as though they *must* find a way to do so.

> "The dead are alive and they try to prove it in many ways. One way they show this is by talking to us through our tape recorders . . . . Recently, one of my daughters had a serious auto accident. She told me the following morning that shortly before the accident she had a strong impression she should not continue on the highway. At the same time there was a purple light around the steering wheel . . .ignoring both . . .she continued on her way. A short time later the accident occurred. When I went to my tape recorder later that morning and asked what the purple light was that my daughter had seen, I was told, "'Mom Wilson was there.' [Mom Wilson had died 3 years earlier]." [15]

This author was fifty years old when I received my first message through an excellent medium. My mother, who had died 13 years earlier, came to me and said, "You are the ones that are dead, you know." The medium's voice had a pedantic air to it, just as my mother used to talk. It was that experience which helped me understand what Jesus meant when he said, *Let the dead bury their dead* (Matt 8:22). But my believing turned to conviction when I heard Archangel Gabriel explain it. What he explained is also found in *A Course in Miracles:* "Yet the Bible says that a deep sleep fell upon Adam, and nowhere is there reference to his waking up. The world has not yet experienced any comprehensive reawakening or rebirth. Such a rebirth is impossible as long as you continue to project or miscreate." [16]

Arthur Conan Doyle
Apparently even those on earth who believe in spiritualism learn to revise their beliefs when they transition to spirit. "Sir Arthur Conan Doyle was – as the world knows – an ardent Spiritualist. After his death in 1930, however, he discovered that many of the Spiritualist beliefs which he himself had sponsored needed revision in the light of his own experience. . . . His family, convinced from the outset that it was he himself who had come back, helped him throughout. This book contains the new revelation of Spiritualism that he made. " [17]

Stewart Edward White, author of *The Unobstructed Universe*, writes on page 16 about *The Betty Book*. After her death, Betty (Stewart's wife), from the spirit world, told her husband:
"The world calls me – us here – dead. But sometimes people, unable to endure the thought of such a blanking out, speak of a loved one as having 'gone on.' That idea, *the act of going on*, is more correctly true. . . . all we 'dead' are changed; glorified with our own immortality.
Even as you, too, will be glorified." [18]

James Pike
James Pike, in his book *The Other Side*, relates many conversations he had with his son who had committed suicide months before. An excerpt from one conversation:
"Don't you ever believe that God can be personalized. He is the Central Force . . . Do you know how exciting it is to come back? To be dead – but we are not the dead ones, you are the dead ones, you are the dead ones, because you are only firing on two cylinders. I want so much to tell you about a world where everybody is out to create a greater sense of love and harmony. A world in which music and color and poetry are all interwoven, making a majestic pattern . . ." [19]

How many times must we hear 'there is no death', centuries after Jesus *proved* it? "It is research such as Dr.Moody presents in his book *Life After Life* that will enlighten many and will confirm what we have been taught for two thousand years – that there is life after death." Elisabeth Kubler-Ross, MD. in Foreword to *Life after Life*.

81

Near Death Experience (NDE)

The Steigers
Brad and Sherry Steiger wrote a book about the NDE of several
children. One such case was about a boy who had been diagnosed as
'hopeless'. One day his mother visited him in the hospital, and
when asked, "Did you dream about angels?" Bobby Owens replied,
"It wasn't a dream, Mommy. . . I was in heaven with angels and lots of
other boys and girls. . ." [20]

Another story told by the Steigers:
Having previously suffered from rheumatic fever and having a NDE,
Sherry had seen angels before. Later, when she was eight years old, an
angel visited her, at a summer camp in Michigan, Sherry had an angel
manifest to her and her friends:

"The angelic being appeared to come down through the ceiling of the
cabin in which Sherry was staying, and most of the startled girls went
down on their knees and folded their hands in prayer." [21]

From page xi of the Foreword to *Angels A to Z,* Andy Lakey describes
his experience after a drug overdose:
"I overdosed on cocaine and knew I was dying . . . With time running
out, I begged repeatedly to live, to stay in this world. . . . I began to feel
a response. Al movement started at my feet. Seven beings swirled up
and enveloped me . . . My body dematerialized as it was lifted to
another place. The images I paint now are echoes of this experience."

NDE and psychic ability
"Numerous researchers have discovered that both adults and children
who are survivors of a near-death experience may develop
extraordinary paranormal abilities . . .
"Dr. P.M.H. Atwater told us that in her extensive research into her
near-death experience she would estimate that seventy percent of those

people who declare themselves to be psychics, clairvoyants, channelers, or otherwise gifted with extrasensory abilities had an NDE as a child." [22]

Automatic Writing

Neale Donald Walsh. "In the spring of 1992 . . . and extraordinary phenomena occurred in my life. God began talking with you through me . . .

"As I scribbled out the last of my bitter, unanswerable questions and prepared to toss my pen aside, my hand remained poised over the paper, as if held there by some invisible force. Abruptly, the pen began *moving on its own.* . . Out came . . .

Do you really want an answer to all these questions, or are you just venting?

"Before I knew it , I had begun a conversation . . . and I was not writing so much as *taking dictation.*" [23]

Automatic writing is just that – the writing instrument moves seemingly on its own --- but does a pen have the ability to think?

"Grace Rosher, who does automatic writing with a pen lying lightly on her hand. Her gift first made itself manifest after her fiancée died when, pausing after finishing a perfectly normal letter, she discovered to her surprise that the pen was moving by itself. The handwriting was that of her dead fiancée, Gordon Burdick." [24]

Ministering of Angels

As time goes by, more and more people are having experiences with angels. Or are there more people willing to tell it? Or are more publishers willing to print it? Excerpts from *The Boy Who Came Back from Heaven:*

"... Five angels were carrying Daddy outside the car.
Four were carrying his body and one was supporting
his neck and head. . . "   p.14

Also, a description of angels:
"They [angels] are completely white and have wings. . ."
p.86

After holy visits from angels, his face revealed a change
in its appearance.
"The angels have visited me many times . . . People
have told me that after I am with the angels my face is
glowing – like a thousand Christmas mornings. . ."
pp. 86-87

Basil Bristow (2009)
Mr. Bristow read one of my books and, in gratitude, sent me a signed
copy of his book, *Bluestone*, published in 2009, containing the first 100
messages of Bluestone.
"I first met Bluestone on Tuesday, November 15th, 2005 while I was in
meditation. He told me that he would like me to channel his messages
and to distribute them to those who asked for them. . . .

"He [Bluestone] told me that he was going to address the subject of
'Universal Consciousness.' . . . I agreed for I had been channeling
various entities since early 2004 . . . I chose the name Bluestone
because of a large piece of blue glass slag that came from the bottom
of a glassblowers vat. I had purchased it a few years before." [25]

The singular focus of all universal souls seems to peace on earth. They
do so by bringing love and merciful acts to those of us in need of
them.

"There is not one universal soul who does not work to bring peace to
the Earth. There is not an angelic being who is not engaged in acts of
mercy to those who face difficulties. And there is not a single Universal
Consciousness thought that does not include love for those who

84

inhabit the Earth . . . but such blessings must be accepted by those on Earth." [26]

Part of Bluestone's lesson 11:
"So, as the morning breaks on Earth today, look for those of us who already stand in your presence, ready to assist in the affairs of the Earth. We are tireless in our desire to help so, at the close of the day, we will not rest for there is much to accomplish.

" Be assured that Earth is a key part of the universe and the consciousness of the universe stands knocking at your portal. Please allow us to enter." [27]

9/11/01
There were plans, shortly after the national tragedy, for the Sci-Fi TV show to record John Edwards giving messages to survivors from their loved ones in spirit. Instead of this being seen as a wonderful opportunity to help heal survivors, some saw this "as extreme tastelessness in search of ratings", and the show was pulled.[28]

Critics of Psychism
One of the criticisms of psychics is that they charge a fee for their 'gift'. For those so gifted (by God) it is often their only means of financial support. Are not doctors, lawyers, architects imbued with gifts of learning? Would anyone say they should not charge a fee? Scripture reports that everyone offering services should be paid, *And in the same house remain, eating and drinking such as they give; for the labourer is worthy of his hire.* (Luke 10:7)

In the UK there was the 1735 Witchcraft Act. It was replaced by the Fraudulent Mediums Act in 1951. Then came the Consumer Protection Act of 2008. The website "Spiritualists Workers' Association warns: "The changes in the legislation are a minefield . . .We have to fight it. If not, we will go back to the Dark Ages, where we will be persecuted and prosecuted."

In the United States, also, psychics must protect themselves from the courts: A psychic on 9/30/11, in Chesterfield County, VA, was denied her right to operate as a psychic "plaintiff's predictions and counseling

85

services are inherently deceptive commercial speech, ... the court also rejected plaintiff's free exercise claims. . . finding that she is not engaged in religious practices. It also rejected her equal protection claims." *Moore-King v. County of Chesterfield Virginia.*

Some famous believers in divination
Some of the famous people who accepted divination were Abraham Lincoln, Thomas Edison, Saint- Saens, Robert Schumann, William James, Margaret Mead. Psychiv Powers, 24-87

Divination in the Future

"The REAL is never seen; the Cause, the Source, the True,
The holiness we crave lies just beyond our view.
The high desires, the good, the love that purifies
Cannot be touched nor seen by these too-human eyes." [29]

Yet the Bible assures us that everything will be shown to us that is now hidden. All will be known and understood. *For nothing is secret, that shall not be made manifest: neither anything hid, that shall not be known and come abroad.* Luke 8:17
To open our minds to the hidden things (which are in spirit) we must accept the idea that faith is the corner stone of that opening. *Now faith is the substance of things hoped for, the evidence of things not seen.* Heb. 11:1

If hope springs eternal then we all have hope of better days. For evidence of things not seen we *must* open our minds to the one means of communication open to us that will provide that evidence. Communication with the spirit world of God will provide that evidence. And that communication is available to us twenty-four seven. Turning our backs on it solves nothing. Opening to it will yield every answer to every question we can imagine. One by one, we can and will fully accept the holy connection we have with our Creator, and then listen carefully as It guides us through every storm. It will never lead us astray. It will never leave us. We will have come home to God in our consciousness, where we began.

"We will gradually see, in the not too distant future, philosophy, science and religion uniting again, as they were united in ancient times in Greece, Egypt, Persia and India . . . then, and only then, a new glorious civilization, a civilization with soul as well as with intellect, will once more arise, surpassing all previous civilizations which have ever flourished on the face of the earth." [30]

CHAPTER 10
COMMUNICATION WITH OTHER LIFE FORMS

Animal Communication
Edgar Cayce's experience
"I prayed very earnestly that afternoon as I sat in the woods by my favorite tree that had so often seemed to speak to me, answering many of my childish questions, as the birds and little animals . . . would gather about me. . . I seemed to hear the answer that God was just as near and personal as we would allow Him to be, speaking to us through His creatures." [1]

Opening ourselves to communication with animals is the only prerequisite to doing so. "When I first heard of communication with animals I thought it might be possible – but only by a gifted mystic. As I began to research this book I heard over and over that *anyone* is potentially able to do it, anyone who is willing to work at it and suspend disbelief." [2]

Psychic animals
"Man is in that position where he may gain the greater lesson from nature, and the creatures in the natural world; they each fulfilling their purpose, singing their song, filling the air with their perfume, that they, too, may honor and praise their Creator." [3]

Psychic Pets
Horses, dogs and cats, have been known to find ways to communicate with humans. "A pet may not always be able to understand or interpret all that it perceives in its owner, but in all cases the psychic realm is modulating and informing your pet's behavior. Whether you choose to or not, you are sending psychic waves which most animals can automatically receive." [4]

There is an amazing story of Abraham Lincoln's dog:
"Many stories are told of animals predicting the impending death of their owners . . . A number of psychics allegedly predicted the assassination of Lincoln, but none more clearly than the president's dog.

"The White House staff made every kind of unsuccessful attempt to quiet the dog when he suddenly went berserk. Although always so quiet and docile, shortly before the tragedy the animal raced around the house in a frenzy and kept up a dirge of unholy howling." [5]

Psychic Plants
"The spirits of nature have various ethereal forms and functions and are known by different names or identities, according to the cultural background of those that perceive them. They are called plant spirits, flower fairies, sprites, elves, gnomes, leprechauns, landscape or mountain devas, angels." [6]

When we realize – and accept – that communication for humans extends to beasts, birds and the plant world, how vast our opportunities become to learn from and share with our co-occupants of the earth plane.

"Now it remains to explore the nature of plants, and in doing so we have finally become aware of their psychic properties. Not only do plants partake of that indestructible element that characterizes man and animal (and perhaps minerals) but there is communication from plant to man and vice versa . . ." [7]

And this communication will nourish us spiritually as we grow in our awareness to the at-one-ment we share with God. The analogy was well expressed by Meister Eckhart:

"The seed of God is in us. Given an intelligent and hard-working farmer, it will thrive and grow up to God, whose seed it is; and accordingly its fruits will be God-nature. Pear seeds grow into pear trees, nut seeds into nut trees, and God seed into God."

Angelic Gardens

Findhorn, in Scotland
In the Foreword of *Findhorn*, William Irwin Thompson wrote: "Modern man knows how to talk back to nature, but he doesn't know how to listen. Archaic man knew how to listen to wind and water,

flower and tree, angel and elf. All the archaic cultures, Tibetan, Hopi, Sufi and Celtic, are returning because they contain the very consciousness we need for the present and the future" [8]

In an amazing demonstration of planting and growing a garden in sand, the founders of Findhorn enjoyed constant communication with the plant world. "The founders of Findhorn were not establishing a set pattern that had to be imitated in order to cooperate with nature. To recreate your bit of earth, you don't need a dynamo like Peter, a channel for God's voice like Eileen, a free spirit like Dorothy to receive advice from the devas, and a wizard like Roc to talk with elementals and nature spirits. . . the essential message is . . .[that] God, the devas and the nature spirits are all aspects of one life." [9]

Even the soil was not conducive to a garden of any kind. ". . .what we had here was sand with a mass of stones and gravel about a foot below." P5

Although Findhorn was blessed to have such gifted gardeners, they made it clear that only a firm faith in the oneness of all life is required to bring a perfect garden into existence. Faith was the foundation of Findhorn. The founders all had it and knew they had to rely on it, together. Because *Findhorn* bears a chapter by each member of Findhorn, we present here an excerpt from each gardener. In reading this fine book, the true meaning of 'community' becomes abundantly clear, as each member of the garden, telling his or her story, often refers to how other members impact on their own gardening experience and spiritual growth.

Peter

Next, I tackled the . . . gorse and brambles . . . Digging
into it, I found nothing more than gravel. There was
hardly even sand. The soil had washed down the slope
and settled between the caravan and the garage. The
only answer was to exchange the two, wheelbarrowing
gravel out, shoveling soil in. This involved an
enormous amount of work, but it had a spiritual as well
as physical effect on the area.
I was told that by working in total concentration and
with love for what I was doing, I could instill light into

the soil. It is difficult to explain, but I was actually aware of radiations of light and love passing through me as I worked. This did not happen until I got a spade in my hands and started digging. [10]

Eileen

We began to realize that everything our bodies were absorbing during this time was of vital importance. That is why we had to eat the produce from our own garden. No artificial fertilizers or insecticides were being used, devas and nature spirits were tending the garden, and all of us were contributing our positive thoughts and vibrations to the plants. *I want you to realize that the produce out of this garden will do you more good than anything bought. It has tremendous life force in it, which is the main thing that you need. This food is blessed by Me.* We developed an entirely new understanding of the purpose of eating. We were told that we were purifying the atomic structure of our bodies, transforming the dense physical substance into light and lightness which would be more receptive to absorbing energies from the sun, sea and air, and would require less solid food." [11]

Dorothy

Dorothy, a college educated Canadian was still seeking answers. She heard a voice within and began writing down the messaged daily. She sought guidance regarding her garden in Scotland. The messages led her to contact the essence of the garden pea, a vegetable she had always enjoyed. A response came from the garden pea deva:

I can s peak to you, human. I am entirely directed by my work which is set out and molded and which I merely bring to fruition, yet you have come straight to my awareness. My work is clear before me – to bring the force fields into manifestation regardless of obstacles, and there are many in this man-infested world. While the vegetable kingdom holds no grudge against those it feeds, man takes what he can as a matter of course, giving no thanks. This makes us strangely hostile." [12]

Several years later, after Findhorn had successfully grown a lovely garden in sandy soil, Dorothy noted the following: "[devas] are part of a whole hierarchy of beings, from the earthiest gnome to the highest archangel, . . . the devas hold the archetypal pattern and plan for all forms around us, and they direct the energy needed for materializing them. The physical bodies of minerals, vegetables, animals and humans are all energy brought into form through the work of the devic kingdom." [13]

Roc

"To anyone who may have expressed a wish to see and talk with nature spirits, whether or not you have dropped a penny into a wishing well, remember it took sixty-three years for my wish to be granted, and don't lose hope. The nature spirits must be believed in with complete sincerity and faith. They must be appreciated and given thanks and love for the work they do. Let us try in our own ways to make friends with these wonderful beings and ask their help in making Earth a beautiful and perfect place." [14]

David

"The role of Findhorn, since its inception, has been to demonstrate communion and cooperation with nature, based on a vision of the life and purposeful intelligence inherent in it. This is an important role, considering that it arises within a Western cultural milieu in which nature has been increasingly quantified as part of an industrial process." [15]

The Garden Today

Learning about how to cooperate with plant life was only part of the learning experience at Findhorn: "What we really have to learn is how to treat the soil as a living entity. The soil is alive but a lot of agricultural practices . . . [are] directed at just reaping its benefit by putting on fertilizers and taking out crops – without respect to the soil itself." [16]

It did not take long for the wonder of Findhorn to reveal itself: "it was starting to attract local attention. People would come to have a look and go away shaking their heads, scarcely able to believe it was only three months since the first seeds were sown. How could there be so much greenness and vitality when all around was dry deadness?" [17]

Hope for all gardeners sprang from the experiences at Findhorn. "To contact the deva world an interchange in word or thought is not necessary. . . Whenever we are in a state of joy, love, lightness, freedom, we are with the devas." [18]

Machine communication
With some imagination and acceptance we can begin to comprehend communication with nature. Even more astounding from the book *Findhorn* is a statement from the Machine Deva: "*Machines, too, respond to human love and care. All of you have had experiences of this but have not usually registered the implications because they seemed nonsensical to the mind. We would not belittle the mind, for through it we were brought to birth. But behind the mind, empowering it, are forces of even greater strength which we would ask you to use when you deal with machines. Metals are part of the one life; treat them as such ad you will get a response. Bring joy to the world of metal by cooperating with us.*" [19]

How could anyone read this and not identify with the love of their own automobile? We often name our cars; we wash and polish them with loving care. At one time Gabriel told me that the angels had named my car. In amazement I asked the name. 'Joy mobile' was the answer. I have often thought of having it painted on both sides of the car, but never did.

Peralandra, in the United States
Machaelle Small Wright wrote a book entitled *Behaving as if the God in All Life Mattered.* After reading about the Findhorn garden in Scotland, she knew that she wanted to establish a garden based on information she received from the plant devas. When she and her husband moved to a wooded area in Virginia, she decided on a name for her garden.

"In 1968 I had read a science fiction book by C.S. Lewis called *Peralandra*. . . a planet that existed in perfection. . .I felt that our woods . . . had not lost the spark of perfection." [20]

93

We dream of a goal, and sometimes the dream seems like it can never be more than a dream. But if we hold it in our thoughts we are able, at some future time, to materialize it.. The greatest drawback We ever encounter is our blindness to what *can be*. Mrs. Wright shares her amazing discovery in *Behaving as if the God in All Life Mattered*.

"I immediately discovered that there is an extraordinary intelligence inherent in all forms of nature – plant, animal and mineral; that contained within this intelligence are the answers to any questions we could possibly have . . . In a recent session with the Overlighting Deva of Perelandra, I [asked], . . .' Why is it seemingly so important for humanity to re-connect spiritually to planet Earth now?'

Answer of The Overlighting Deva:
"I would emphasize to you the word 'survival' in answering a question such as this. . . You see survival as the opposite of death. We don't recognize death as a reality. . . By survival, we mean the act of maintaining the fusion and balance between spirit and matter on the physical planet Earth". [21]

Others have sensed, and written about, the feeling nature of plant life. "Jerry Baker, expert gardener, says, 'In my opinion, based on experience, plants do have feeling and will produce for someone they like and be stubborn for someone they dislike." [22]

It is said that there is nothing new under the sun, but there is definitely much old that we must open our minds to under the sun. And when we do so, life will take on a new lightness and beauty to which we have been blind for centuries, if not eons.

Vibration of Crystals

"In man's unending quest for knowledge of self, he is rediscovering the ancient sciences and the lost arts which actually were never really lost. Much of the ancient information was either not widely known by the general public or was secretly practiced by a select few . . . . The hidden value of crystals, as well as other natural stones and gems, was recognized by what we have come to think of as 'primitive man,' and they have once again only begun to surface in the light of recent developments in alternative thinking. . . .In addition to being really fun to own, they bring their owner success, good fortune, love, and a wealth of other benefits." [23]

Some healers work exclusively with gemstones. I once received a treatment for a painful hip. Guided by spirit, she placed various gems and crystals around my body as I lay on my back. The top of my head, my chest and at my feet were some of the locations where she placed the gemstones. The healing helped for a short time, but I finally required surgery for a total hip replacement.

Minerals and history
If we can communicate with machinery, it is not much of a stretch to accept communication with minerals.

> ". . . the essence of the communication from plants tends to be in the 'now,' without reference to history. Minerals bridge time. They use the same form for centuries, even eons, and when we touch into the intelligence, it's quite possible for us to experience a particular historical period or event that is contained with the 'memory bank;' of this specific mineral. For example, a woman in one of my workshops chose to get in touch with the consciousness of a stone she had picked up on a beach in Ireland . . . the stone gave her a gift -- a gift of joy . . . it flashed the woman into an idyllic beach scene where many children were playing and having a wonderful time, and the woman was enveloped with a sensation of joy . . .But the scene wasn't contemporary. It was actually a scene that had occurred in the late 1800s on a beach in Holland --- which was where this stone was sitting until being washed to the shores of Ireland." [24]

God is the Creator of all life. There is life in all mammals and all vegetation, as we have explained above. A more basic view is possible when we look at the four basic elements of earth: air, fire and water:

Air: We are spiritual beings because we are God's children and we live by the breath of life. Without air we cannot live. Air is the vehicle through which all mental telepathy travels as well as being the vehicle for accessing the Akashic Records.

Earth: provides us with the plant life which communicates with those of us willing to listen. Divining rods are used by anyone seeking water or minerals under the ground.

Fire: We describe an example of fire mediumship in Part II.

Water: Mr. Emoto in Japan discovered that water responds to human thought. His book describing this communication is entitled, *Messages from Water* (1999). He wrote several other books based on his numerous experiments. In one of his experiments a group of people surrounded a pond that was highly polluted. They prayed and sent loving thoughts to the pond over time. Eventually, the pond became clean and clear.

Personal Channeling
" . . . an individual may be said to be psychic to the degree that he is able to put aside the distracting input from the conscious and subconscious in preference to input from the super conscious, which may put him in touch with all worthwhile information. For a channel to be consistently accurate and helpful, then, one must be able to tap the super conscious on a regular basis." [25]

When one sees channeling as some kind of 'evil' the door is shut against learning anything except what the five senses teach us. And they teach us nothing. They offer to us a perception – our own personal idea of how things should be. Gabriel told us that perception is deception. Our senses all deceive us. They are limited, for one thing. Sounds exist which we cannot hear. We are unable to see around corners, some odors overwhelm us, some feelings render us unconscious. True perception is the eternal truth of existence. We can only know it by revelation. Revelation is not limited to Bible personalities. Every 'hunch', every 'gut feeling', every answer that comes to us from an unseen source is a revelation. In scripture we find an example of how revelation works:

But whom say ye that I am?
And Simon Peter answered and said, Thou art the Christ, the Son of the living
God.
And Jesus answered and said unto him, Blessed at thou, Simon Barjona: for flesh
and blood hath not revealed it unto thee, but my Father which is in heaven. Matt
16:15-17

Every truth can be known, every question can be answered. When we
say 'I don't know,' we are refusing to accept the idea that we *can know*.
We are all children of the living God. We are created in His image,
which is spirit. We need only knock, to have it opened unto us. We
need only ask, and we shall find the answer. We must first seek to
know. *For everyone that asketh receiveth; and he that seeketh findeth; and to him*
that knocketh it shall be opened. Matt 7:8

Yes, everyone ---- not the apostles only; not the seventy sent out by
Jesus; not the 144 who followed after him; but everyone.

Edgar Cayce on Channeling your Higher Self:
"Channeling is basically a creative process. Cayce's formula of creation:
'Spirit is the Life, Mind is the Builder, Physical is the result,' . . . The
formula for channeling becomes, 'Set the ideal, then set oneself aside
to let the idealized spirit express itself.' The result is an inspiration and
then an action that serves the ideal." [26]

Fulfillment of Prophecy
How can prophecy be verified, understood, and accepted, without a
firm foundation of truth? For centuries we have accepted the literal
words of the King James' version of the Judeo-Christian Bible.
The original Bible was written in Hebrew and Greek. Back then,
scribes were rare, and translators even more rare. These were all
talented men who probably did their best, but it is highly unlikely that
anyone 'proofread' their work. Now Archangel Gabriel has come to
open our eyes to the truth of the original words. There was no literary
excellence two thousand years ago. Two profound errors of translation
are in Scripture, as explained by Archangel Gabriel:

1. Jesus Christ is described as the 'only begotten son of God' in the
gospel according to John four times, in Paul's letter to the Hebrews
once and in I John once. Yet, the original words were "Jesus Christ,

97

begotten son of the only God". This brings an entirely different meaning to the words. Gabriel said the entire human family is the only begotten son of God.

2. When on the cross, Jesus is reported to have said (in Matt. 27:46 and Mark 15:34) "My God, my God, why hast thou forsaken me?" Gabriel explained that what Jesus actually said was, "My Sun, My Sun, why hast thou forsaken me?"

Firstly, there is a small diacritical mark in the original script, which is the difference between 'God' and 'Sun', that translators erred in noting. Secondly, it is noted in scripture that the sky darkened for three hours at the time of the crucifixion, and Jesus was questioning why the Sun failed to shine. And finally, how could anyone honestly accept the idea that Jesus doubted his Father in Heaven? If those biblical words were true, they would seriously undermine all previous words of faith proclaimed by Jesus. With these *correct* translations we can readily accept the one lesson that Archangel Gabriel came to deliver: You are all children of God; wake up to that fact and live from the Lord God of your Being.

This is the accepted time to awaken to the divine truth. "Now is the time of prophecy fulfilled. *Now are all ancient promises upheld and fully kept . . . Sit silently and wait upon your Father. He has willed to come to you when you have recognized it is your will He do so. And you could never have come this far unless you saw, however dimly, that it is your will.*" [27]

As humanity opens its mind to accepting all these forms of divination, a broad spectrum of new experiences will illuminate the days. We will accept the oneness of the life in the universe. We will accept the oneness of the human family and the oneness of the human family with God our Creator. Walls separating religions will fall; walls separating groups of people will melt. Love will have conquered hate and trust and openness will prevail. This is the Heaven on Earth that we all privately seek but currently prevent as we continue to be blind to the God within. We all are children of God. We all are lights of the world. Now, after centuries of dark ignorance, it is time to employ the methods which shall awaken us --- explained so clearly by Jesus the Christ.

Some of Gabriel's and Jesus' teachings, through time, include:
Honor who you are; love yourself. Love thy neighbor as thyself, for we are all of one family on Earth. Forgive everyone, for every wound inflicted is by your own choice. Seek the kingdom of God, which is within. It has been there since God created you, remains there now and abides until the end of time.

Our awakening awaits us. We each have the ability to awaken to the God within. Now is the time to use that ability, for we have spent too much time believing in illusions, too much energy looking outwardly for redemption, too much dreaming of Heaven, unaware it resides within. William James put it so well: "Compared to what we ought to be, we are half awake."

PART TWO
KINDS OF DIVINATION

CHAPTER 11
MENTAL MEDIUMSHIP

Introduction
The historical comparison of supernatural events is more meaningful
when shown by kinds of divination. Hopefully, this method is clearer
to the reader as the following pages report the various methods of
divination found through the centuries. The following examples are
divided into physical and mental phenomena. For a complete list of
psychic phenomena in Scripture, the reader is directed to the
Appendix. It was the first sight of that list which prompted the writing
of this book.

Clairvoyance (seeing spirit)

Gen. 15:1
*After these things the word of the Lord came unto Abram in a vision, saying, Fear
not, Abram: I am thy shield, and thy exceeding great reward.*

Luke 24:30-31
  *And it came to pass, as he sat at meat with them, he took bread, and blessed it,
and brake, and gave to them.*
  *And their eyes were opened, and they knew him; and he vanished out of their
sight.*

It is rare to find a scientist who accepts divination. In 1940 it was even
more rare. In 1940, Mr. Forman wrote: "In these scientific modern
times . . . virtually no one believes in prophecy . . . Yet an eminent
biologist like Dr. Alexis Carrel, among the foremost in the world, . . .
quite simply informs us that he has been interested in the phenomena
of telepathy and clairvoyance in the same manner that he has been
interested in physiology, chemistry and pathology; and that both
telepathy and clairvoyance are a normal, although rare, activity of the
human being." [1]

Swedenborg

W. F. Prince, in his book Noted *Witnesses for Psychic Occurrences,* four instances of Swedenborg's experiences are given. One, probably the most well-known, is the day that he 'saw' in his mind's eye, a fire near his home in Stockholm while having dinner at a friend's home in Gottenberg (300 miles distant). Three days later the fire, its specific destruction, and the time of its extinguishment all precisely agreed with Swedenborg's vision. pp46-55. Immanuel Kant gathered information regarding the fire and reported it the same. [2]

". . . From that day I gave up the study of all worldly science and labored in spiritual things, according as the Lord opened my eyes, very often daily, so that in midday I could see into the other world, and in a state of perfect wakefulness converse with angels and spirits." [3]

Swedenborg also predicted the Russian emperor's death:
"In the year 1762, on the very day when Peter III of Russian died, Swedenborg . . . said, "Now, at this very hour, the Emperor Peter III has died in prison --- explaining the nature of his death . . . The papers soon after announced the death of the Emperor, which had taken place on the very same day." [4]

Rudolph Steiner

"When he was a boy . . . he became strangely aware of the presence of living beings who seemed invisible to the eyes of others. Some solitary children do develop an inner world of fantasy but Steiner's world seemed to have been one of direct perception rather than of imagination, for he was a realistic boy, gifted with an exact sense of order and a talent for mathematics." [5]

"[Rudolph} Steiner sees two forces perpetually at work in all evolution: the force that holds back . . . and a force *from outside the earth* that lifts the mind towards higher and higher consciousness and freedom . . ." [6]

Edgar Cayce

Cayce relates his first vision at age fourteen:
> "Kneeling by my bed that night, I prayed again that
> God would show me that He loved me, that He would
> give me the ability to do something for my fellow man

which would show to them His love, even as the
actions of His little creatures in the woods showed me
their trust in one who loved them. . . .I was not yet
asleep when the vision first began . . . A glorious light
as of the rising morning sun seemed to fill the whole
room, and a figure appeared at the foot of my bed. . . .
an angel, or what, I knew not; but gently, patiently, it
said, 'Thy prayers are heard. You will have you wish.
Remain faithful. Be true to yourself. Help the sick, the
afflicted." [7]

Arthur Ford
"Arthur Ford was one of the best-known trance mediums of this
century. He was the man who communicated the great Houdini's last
message to the world [from spirit]; he was the medium through whom
Bishop Pike spoke to his dead son . . . " [8]

Many people have reported seeing their loved ones after their passing.

"The universal experience of apparitions has found its way into the
language and folklore of cultures all over the world, from a time long
before the beginning of recorded history. . . A number of studies
published in medical journals and other scholarly sources have
established that a high percentage of bereaved persons have visions of
the deceased . . . as many as 66% of widows experience apparitions of
their departed husbands." [9]

Sometimes those in spirit choose to reveal themselves in a photo taken
after their death. Mary Todd Lincoln, as a widow, appeared for a
formal photo incognito (veiled in mourning). When the print was
taken, the photographer recognized an apparition standing behind Mrs.
Lincoln as the late president. "Mary Lincoln agreed, and added, "I am
his widow'." [10]

Jesus the Christ speaks to the Essenes
"I need some time to be alone, to compare the path I
have taken with the one that still lies ahead of me. A
father does not make of his son a device to carry out
his plans. Therefore, in giving me a man's body, my

celestial Father gave me a man's freedom as well. This is a sign of love that you must understand. The two hands of the human creature, the choice open to him in the making of his life here on Earth are the first fruits of his oncoming grandeur, more than you can imagine. Strip these ideas of the words that cover them. I show you a pathway for humanity. Looking at the times that are to come, I fear one thing: that which is not understood gives rise to terror, fanaticism, or a withering devotion. So I tell you, do not make a god of me." [11]

Counseling

Ex. 4:15

And thou shalt speak unto him, and put words in his mouth: and I will be with thy mouth, and with his mouth, and will teach you what ye shall do.

Gen. 44:5

Is not this it in which my lord drinketh, and whereby indeed he divineth?

I Sam 9:15-16

Now the Lord had told Samuel in his ear a day before Saul came, saying,
To morrow about this time I will send thee a man out of the land of Benjamin, and thou shalt anoint him that he may save my people out of the hand of he Philistines: for I have looked upon my people, because their cry has come unto me.

Luke 21:14-15

Settle it therefore in your hearts, not to meditate before what ye shall answer:
For I will give you a mouth and wisdom, which all your adversaries shall not be able to gainsay nor resist.

John 4:23-24

But the hour cometh, and now is, when the true worshippers shall worship the Father in spirit and in truth: for the Father seeketh such to worship him.
God is a Spirit: and they that worship him must worship him in spirit and in truth.

Acts 9:17

And Ananais went his way, and entered into the house; and putting his hands on him said, Brother Saul, the Lord, even Jesus, that appeared unto thee in the way as thou camest, hath sent me, that thou mightest receive thy sight, and e filled with the Holy Ghost.

Levi
"And Jesus preached to them the gospel of goodwill, and peace on earth.
He told them of the brotherhood of life, and of the inborn powers of man, and of the kindgom of the soul." [12]

"And Jesus said, Whatever tends to purity in thought, and word, and deed will cleanse the temple of the flesh.
"There are no rules that can apply to all, for men are specialists in sin; each has his own besetting sin.
"And each must study for himself how he can best transmute his tendency to evil things to that of righteousness and love.
"Until men reach the higher plane, and get away from selfishness, this rule will give the best results:
"Do unto other men what you would have them do to you." [13]

The Voice Celestial
"Retain thy faith in thy true self alone;
In thee is Father, Mother and the Son,
In thee the Lord thy God, the Lord is One.
For this I came, for this I go away
That you be born again. This is the day
That your divided selves find unity,
Embraced with the allness of the Me.[14]

Independent Spirit Voice (Clairaudience)

Gen 15:1
After these things the word of the Lord came unto Abram in a vision, saying, Fear not, Abram: I am thy shield, and thy exceeding great reward.

I Sam 8:7 and 8:22 – 'The Lord spoke to Samuel' indicates that the prophet was clairaudient.

Gen 46:2-4
And God spake unto Israel in the visions of the night, and said, Jacob, Jacob. And he said Here I am.
And he said, I am God, the God of thy father: fear not to go down into to Egypt; for I will there make of thee a great nation:
I will go down with thee into Egypt; and I will also surely bring thee up again: and Joseph shall put his hand upon thine eyes.

Matt 17:5
While he yet spake, behold, a bright cloud overshadowed them: and behold a voice out of the cloud, which said, This is my beloved Son, in whom I am well pleased; hear ye him.

John 12:30
Father, glorify thy name. Then came there a voice from heaven, saying, I have both glorified it, and will glorify it again.
The people therefore, that stood by, and heard it, said that it thundered: others said, An angel spake to him.
Jesus answered and said, This voice came not because of me, but for your sakes.

Acts 10:13-16
And there came a voice to him, Rise, Peter; kill, and eat.
But Peter said, Not so, Lord; for I have never eaten anything that is common or unclean.
And the voice spake unto him again the second time, What God hath cleansed, that call not thou uncommon.

Jesus the Christ speaks to the Essenes

"I need some time to be alone, to compare the path I have taken with the one that still lies ahead of me. A father does not make of his son a device to carry out his plans. Therefore, in giving me a man's body, my celestial Father gave me a man's freedom as well. This is a sign of love that you must understand. The two hands of the human creature, the choice open to him in the making of his life here on Earth are the first fruits of his oncoming grandeur, more than you can imagine. Strip these ideas of the words that cover them. I show you a pathway for humanity. Looking at the times that are to come, I fear one thing: that which is not understood gives rise to terror, fanaticism, or a withering devotion. So I tell you, do not make a god of me." [15]

". . . He [Swedenborg] devoted himself to scientific studies and philosophical reflections . . . From 1743 to1745 he entered a transitional phase. . . science and philosophy to theology. Throughout the rest of his life he maintained that this shift was brought about by Jesus Christ, who appeared to him, called him to a new mission, and opened his perception to a permanent dual consciousness of this life and the life after death." [16]

Joan of Arc

Because so much has been written about Joan of Arc, the life she lived and the power she derived from spirit at such an early age, she has remains famous to all future generations. "She came, with powers and genius which should be the marvel of the world while the world stands. She redeemed a nation, she wrought such works as seemed to her people, and well might seem, miraculous. . ." [17]

However, soon after Joan of Arc died, the pope issued a pronouncement against 'witches'. Not only those who prophesied, but even those who predicted the weather!

Only six years after Joan of Arc died, a papal bull (official letter) was issued:
"In 1437 and 1445, Pope Eugene IV issued bulls commanding punishment of witches who caused bad weather, and in 1484 the bull *Summis Desiderantes*, by Pope Innocent VIII, started a wave of torture and execution in which many scores of thousands were killed. Similar bulls we issued by Julius II and Adrian VI. Nor did the Reformation put an end to the terror. Luther joined in the denunciation of witches and there were many executions in protestant Scotland in the seventeenth century." [18]

The strongest condemnation of 'witchcraft' came from Pope Innocent VIII, when he supported a writing entitled *Witches Hammer*, a book containing detailed steps in how to torture and kill those who dared to prophesy or even deny that demons existed. This author held an English translation in hand at a used book store in Saratoga County, NYS. I felt a strong desire to replace it on the shelf and to not even put it in my home bookcase.

Papal support was given to Kramer and 'Sprenger against witchcraft: *Malleus maleficarum* (1489) was their treatise describing the manifestation of witchcraft and also prescribing answers to those who doubted the existence of devils and demons." [19]

Robert Schumann

"I must tell you a presentiment I have had; it haunted me from the 24th to the 27th of March, during which I was absorbed in my new compositions.

"There was a certain passage which obsessed me, and someone seemed to be repeating to me from the depths of his heart: *Ach Gott* (O, my God!) While composing I visualized funeral things, coffins, sorrowing faces. . . When I had finished, I sought for a title. The only which came to my mind was *Leichenphantasie* (Funeral Fantasy) . . . I was so overcome that the tears came to my eyes; I truly did not know why; . . . Then came Therese's letter, and all was clear. Her . . . sister in law's brother had just died."

"Schumann gave the title *Nachtstucke* (Nocturne) to that suite." [20]

James Pike

James Pike, in his book *The Other Side*, relates many conversations he had with his son who had committed suicide months before. An excerpt from one conversation:

"Don't you ever believe that God can be personalized. He is the Central Force . . . Do you know how exciting it is to come back? To be dead – but we are not the dead ones, you are the dead ones, you are the dead ones, because you are only firing on two cylinders. I want so much to tell you about a world where everybody is out to create a greater sense of love and harmony. A world in which music and color and poetry are all interwoven, making a majestic pattern . . ." [21]

Saint Germain
"The thirty-three Discourses contained in this Book were dictated over a *visible* Light and Sound Ray in our home during 1932, by the Ascended Master Saint Germain and those other Ascended Masters directly concerned with this Activity. The sound of His Voice was physically audible to everyone in the room. At times His Visible, Tangible Presence also stood within the room — when He radiated the Power and Energy of the Light Rays to accomplish special wok." [22]

Judy Boss
In her book *In Silence They Return*, Judy opens the Introduction as follows:
"Death is not really the end," I said to my neighbor shortly after my husband was killed, leaving me with five small children to raise alone. "For him, it is an exciting new adventure." And for me life is a challenge that I have to face. I have no time for tears."

After receiving a message from her husband, then in spirit, she said to his heard but unseen self, "Thank you, Mac, Not only have you given me a meaningful philosophy for our children to be raised with, but you have left me with proof of your existence." [23]

Mia Dolan
Mia Dolan is now one of England's best known psychics.
"She was twenty-two when she first heard a voice she could not explain. She had always considered herself to be a down-to-earth person and certainly never believed in psychic phenomena . . . Finally, Mia discovered that she had a rare psychic gift and learned how to control and use it." [24]

Jesus the Christ (1986)
From Jesus the Christ himself, through "Virginia", in 1986: "This is my own statement sent directly to you, not mere reports of my sayings and actions recorded later by the disciples . . .My words are not intended just for so-called Christians but for everyone.
These words address the immediate conditions that your earthly negativity has caused and which must change if you are to prevent serious repercussions. They are serious because I love you and would call your attention to the emergency state in which you reside." [25]

Basil Bristow

In 2010 the author received a signed copy of *Bluestone* after Mr. Bristow read one of my books sent to him by a friend of his as a gift. In 2009, Basil Bristow published a book of Bluestones first 100 messages. "I first met Bluestone on Tuesday, November 15th, 2005 while I was in meditation. He told me that he would like me to channel his messages and to distribute them to those who asked for them.

"He [Bluestone] told me that he was going to address the subject of 'Universal Consciousness.' . . . I agreed for I had been channeling various entities since early 2004 . . . I chose the name Bluestone because of a large piece of blue glass slag that came from the bottom of a glassblowers vat. I had purchased it a few years before." [26]

"There is not one universal soul who does not work to bring peace to the Earth. There is not an angelic being who is not engaged in acts of mercy to those who face difficulties. And there is not a single Universal Consciousness thought that does not include love for those who inhabit the Earth . . . but such blessings must be accepted by those on Earth." [27]

Part of Bluestone's lesson 11:
"So, as the morning breaks on Earth today, look for those of us who already stand in your presence, ready to assist in the affairs of the Earth. We are tireless in our desire to help so, at the close of the day, we will not rest for there is much to accomplish.

"Be assured that Earth is a key part of the universe and the consciousness of the universe stands knocking at your portal. Please allow us to enter." [28]

Jesus the Christ speaks to the Essenes
"I need some time to be alone, to compare the path I have taken with the one that still lies ahead of me. A father does not make of his son a device to carry out his plans. Therefore, in giving me a man's body, my celestial Father gave me a man's freedom as well. This is a sign of love that you must understand. The two hands of the human creature, the choice open to him in

109

the making of his life here on Earth are the first fruits
of his oncoming grandeur, more than you can imagine.
Strip these ideas of the words that cover them. I show
you a pathway for humanity. Looking at the times that
are to come, I fear one thing: that which is not
understood gives rise to terror, fanaticism, or a
withering devotion. So I tell you, do not make a god of
me." [29]

Independent Spirit Writing (Automatic Writing)

Ex 31:18
*And he gave unto Moses, when he had made an end of communing with him upon
the mount Sinai, two tables of testimony, tables of stone, written with the finger of
God.*

Daniel 5:5
*In the same hour came forth fingers of a man's hand, and wrote over against the
candlestick upon the plaister of the wall of the king's palace: and the king saw the
part of the hand that wrote.*

Arthur Ford
Shortly after the death of Arthur Ford, renowned psychic, his close
friend Ruth Montgomery wrote:
"No sooner had I murmured my usual prayer for protection and
placed my fingers in touch-typing position than the [automatic] writing
began:
"Ruth, this is Lilly and the group. Arthur Ford is here and wants you to
know that he is as young as the merry month of May. He feels great
and does not want you to grieve. He is so glad to be here, more
delighted than you will ever know . . ." [30]

Neale Donald Walsh
"In the spring of 1992 . . . and extraordinary phenomena occurred in
my life. God began talking with you through me . . .

"As I scribbled out the last of my bitter, unanswerable questions and
prepared to toss my pen aside, my hand remained poised over the

paper, as if held there by some invisible force. Abruptly, the pen began *moving on its own. . .* Out came . . .

"Do you really want an answer to all these questions, or are you just venting?

"Before I knew it, I had begun a conversation . . . and I was not writing so much as *taking dictation.*"[31]

"Grace Rosher, who does automatic writing with a pen lying lightly on her hand. Her gift first made itself manifest after her fiancé died when, pausing after finishing a perfectly normal letter, she discovered to her surprise that the pen was moving by itself. The handwriting was that of her dead fiancé, Gordon Burdick."[32]

Trance

Num. 24:4
He hath said, which heard the words of God, which saw the vision of the Almighty, falling into a trance, but having his eyes open:

Acts 10:10
And he became very hungry, and would have eaten: but while they made ready, he fell into a trance.

Mesmer
"Just six years after Swedenborg's death a Viennese doctor, Anton Mesmer, arrived in Paris – creating a furor by his teachings and his cures. He seemed to possess a remarkable power, -- placing his subjects in a trance-like condition, in which state many extraordinary phenomena were alleged to have occurred." (*Story of Psychic Science*, p.39). This was the beginning of what is now known as Mesmerism. Out of Mesmerism came Hypnotism, named by Dr. James Braid in 1842.[33]

Levi

111

Scripture omits several years of Jesus' life, for reasons unknown. From the age of twelve, when he was found in the Temple, until his appearance at the Jordan River to be baptized by John, we have no information about the Master's whereabouts or activities. In the twentieth century we were blessed to find a book entitled *The Aquarian Gospel of Jesus the Christ,* which was given to Levi by spirit early in the 20th century. It describes Jesus' journey throughout the known world. At a feast In Persia, he was asked about the devil and hell-fires. His answer was:

"Whatever God, the One, has made is good, and like the great First Cause, the seven spirits all are good, and everything that comes from their creative hands is good.

"Now, all created things have colours, tones and forms their own; but certain tones, though good and pure themselves, when mixed, produce inharmonies, discordant tones.

"And certain things, though good and pure, when mixed, produced discordant things, yea, poisonous things, that men call evil things.

"So evil is the inharmonious blending of the colours, tones, or forms of good.

"Now, man is not all-wise, and yet has will his own. He has the power, and he uses it, to mix God's things in a multitude of ways, and every day he makes discordant sounds, and evil things.

"And every tone and form, be it of good, or ill, becomes a living thing, a demon, sprite, or spirit of a good or vicious kind.

"Man makes his devil thus; and then becomes afraid of him and flees; his devil is emboldened, follows him away and casts him into torturing fires.

"The devil and the burning fires are both the works of
man, and none can put the fires out and dissipate the
evil one, but man who made them both." [34]

Andrew Jackson Davis
"His [Davis] chief work, *Nature's Divine Revelation*, was written in
1846", two years before the birth of U.S. spiritualism by the Fox
Sisters. According to Abebooks.com this book was channeled from
spirit to Davis while he was in a trance.

Inspirational Spirit Writing

Mark 13:11
*But when they shall lead you, and deliver you up, take no thought beforehand what
ye shall speak, neither do ye premeditate: but whatsoever shall be given you in that
hour, that speak ye: for it is not ye that speak, but the Holy Ghost.*

Acts 2:4
*And they were all filled with the Holy Ghost, and began to speak with other
tongues, as he Spirit gave them utterance.*

Edgar Cayce
From EC on ESP: "It has been estimated that during his lifetime
Edgar Cayce spoke in some two dozen different languages while giving
readings, although he had conscious knowledge only of English. [35]

The Author
This writer, as a newly ordained minister, was assigned to give the
Sunday sermon on alternate weeks. The first few sermons given were
based on written notes I made and took to the podium with me. One
day as I began to prepare notes, something told me I did not need to
do that. I always listen to spirit, and so I did not write notes. As usual, I
read from Scripture for a sermon focus. After that I silently said, "OK,
you better guide me here." And I was guided.

After the sermon, I bid farewell to the congregation at the front door,
as was the custom. A young man came up to me and said, "I bet that
sermon took a long time to prepare." I was surprised and said, "No,
not really," Afterward I realized that I had never seen that young man

before – and I never saw him afterward. I am convinced he was an angel, come to remind me how easy it is to depend on spirit. I have been an inspired speaker ever since.

It is essential to note that everyone is an inspired speaker at times. How often has someone we know – or even a stranger sometimes – told us something that distresses them that is very personal or intimate. The story shocks us, but we say something back to them, which *always* seems to help. Some unseen guide provides us with the words.

In the year 2004, as I completed my second book - my memoirs - Jesus the Christ came to me through a dedicated medium and told me that my third book would be a book of meditations, drawn from Scripture, The Course (*A Course in Miracles*) and my own experiences. He said that he would guide me. Not only did he guide me in writing that third book, but guidance continued for the rest of my writing career.

Séances

The Old Testament provides an early description of a séance. The reader is invited to review the 28th Chapter of I Samuel for details of an ancient séance.

The earliest séances became well-known for trumpet sounds, rappings and the turning of he séance table as methods of divining information from those passed on into spirit. But later the psychics began receiving messages, eliminating the need for interpretation of rappings and tiltings.

"The raps, table turnings, and blasts of seance trumpets faded away with the beginning of the 20th century, and in their place messages began to appear. Spoken or written, they conveyed often precise, evidential information apparently from those who had died. Much more difficult to prove fraudulent than physical manifestations, they were also much harder to explain away." [36]

A séance provided such information early in the 20th century and information received at the séance was proven in a court of law:

An airplane [R101] crash of 1930 drew world wide attention. Only in a séance could technical information be learned to explain the cause of the crash. This information was later confirmed by engineers:
"This Court [of Inquiry] started its work on October 28, three weeks after the memorable séance with Eileen Garrett. Much of the technical information given then by the airship's captain was confirmed during the inquiry, and would not have been available to the public before the séance. [37]

Mr. Charlton, who had been involved in the construction of R101, read a copy of the séance report and described it as "an astounding document" as it contained more than 40 highly technical and confidential details of what occurred on the fatal flight. As confirmation, he stated, ". . . that for anyone present at the séance to have obtained information beforehand was grotesquely absurd." [38]

Spirit Communication in Dreams

Gen. 37:10
And he told it to his father, and to his brethren: and his father rebuked him, and said unto him, What is this dream that thou hast dreamed? Shall I and thy mother and thy brethren indeed come to bow down ourselves to thee to the earth?

Matt. 27:19
When he was set down on the judgment seat, his wife sent unto him, saying, Have thou nothing to do with that just man: for I have suffered many things this day in a dream because of him.

It must be impossible to describe a personal experience with angels, or to tell another in feeble words what Heaven is like, after visiting it. But we are blessed with some feeble words of Swedenborg when he attempted to tell us of his experience.

        ". . . The idea at once struck me how great the grace of
        the Lord is, who accounts and appropriates to us our

resistance to temptation, though it is purely God's grace and is His and not our work; and He overlooks our weaknesses in it, which yet must be manifold . .
.Afterward I awoke and slept again many times and all was in answer to my thoughts, yet so that in everything there was such life and glory that I can give no description of it; for it was all heavenly, clear to me at the time, but afterward inexpressible. In short I was in heaven, and I heard a language which no human tongue can utter with its inherent life, nor the glory and inmost delight resulting from it. Besides, while I was awake I was in a heavenly ecstasy which is also indescribable. . . Praise and honor and glory be to the Highest! Hallowed be His Name! Holy, Holy, Lord God of Hosts!" [39]

Susan B. Anthony
"Mrs. Stanton wrote in her diary:

In a few days we are expecting Miss Anthony to make us a visit. She has had a very remarkable dream. The physician ordered her from Philadelphia to Atlantic City for her health. While in the latter place, she had a very vivid dream one night. She thought she was being burnt alive in one of the hotels, and when she arose in the morning, told her niece what she had dreamed. "We must pack at once and go back to Philadelphia," she said. This was done, and the next day the hotel in which they had been, ten other hotels and miles of the boardwalk, were destroyed by fire." [40]

Elizabeth Cady Stanton
" . . . At Washington, at a time when Congress was sitting . . . [Stanton] . . . was told the house [hotel] was full. After some hesitation the clerk, observing her distress, undertook, if she would wait half an hour, that a room . . . should be got ready for her. . . She went to bed early and slept soundly till she was awakened by the sensation of a hand touching her face, and a voice cried, with a piteous accent, 'Oh, Mother! Mother!' She determined to go to sleep again, and succeeded. Again she was awakened with the hand nervously stroking her face and the blood-curdling cry, 'Oh, Mother! Mother!

It was no use trying to sleep. . . As soon as she heard
the servants moving she rang the bell and the
chambermaid came in with startled look. To her the
visitor related her experiences.

"Yes, marm,' said the chambermaid, "I told them they
ought not to have put you in the room. He was only
carried out an hour before you came."

"Who was carried out?" said the lady.

"Why, the young man who has been lying here for a
fortnight in delirium tremens and died. He was
stretching out his hands, feeling for something, and
crying in heartbreaking voice, 'Oh, Mother! Mother!'" [41]

Rebecca Ruter Springer

From her book, *Intra Muros*, Rebecca speaks of her experience 'on the
other side,' which she visited while in a three –year coma:

"Then the Savior began to speak, and the sweetness of
his voice was far beyond the melody of the heavenly
choir. And his gracious words! Would that I could,
would that I dared, transcribe them as they fell from his
lips. Earth has no language by which I could convey
their lofty meaning. He first touched lightly upon the
earth-life, and showed so wonderfully the link of light
uniting the two lives – the past with the present. Then
he unfolded to us some of the earlier mysteries of the
blessed life, and pointed out the joyous duties just
before us.

"When he ceased, we sat with bowed heads as he
withdrew. Our hearts were so enfolded, our souls so
uplifted, our spirits so exalted, our whole being so
permeated with his divinity, that when we arose we left
the place silently and reverently, each bearing away a
heart filled with higher, more divine aspirations, and
clearer views of the blessed life upon which we were
permitted to enter." [42]

Intra muros was republished in 1994 with the title *Into the
Light*.

Queen Victoria
Queen Victoria, ruler of England for over 60 years, found solace in knowing her husband was alive in spirit. Queen Victoria's personal manservant, John Brown, "reportedly was also a medium who enabled the widowed Queen to communicate with her beloved Albert. The evidence for Brown's mediumship is mixed, but the Queen certainly believed that he had genuine premonitions of the future, and relied on him greatly." [43]

John Brown was not the only medium who brought Queen Victoria comforting words from her deceased husband.

"According to his daughter, Eva Lee, Robert James Lee was only 13 or 14 when he delivered his first spirit message to Queen Victoria from Prince Albert. Miss Lees says the messages went on until the Queen's death." [44]

Spirit Guidance

Dan. 6:22
My God hath sent his angel, and hath shut the lions' mouths , that they have not hurt me: forasmuch as before him innocency was found in me; and also before thee, O king, have I done no hurt.

Acts 11:12
And the spirit bade me go with them, nothing doubting. Moreover these six brethren accompanied me, and we entered into the man's house:
And he shewed us how he had seen an angel in his house, which stood and said unto him, Send men to Joppa, and call for Simon, whose surname is Peter;

Jesus speaks
"These sayings are sent for the Elect Ones, His Servants. They are from the Faithful and True One, even Adonai. To-day they are restored that His Christs may understand who it is who speaketh again unto them; who they themselves were and are; what they once more were about to become; and the profound and vital part they are to take in the New Age and the restored true Drama of the Soul and the Planet." [45]

118

Cayce

"The 'sleeping' Edgar Cayce was . . . a psychic known to thousands of people, in all walks of life, who had cause to be grateful for his help. Indeed, many of them believed that he alone had either 'saved' or 'changed' their lives when all seemed lost. . . .[he] was a medical diagnostician, a prophet, and a devoted proponent of Bible lore." [46]

St. Germain

From the Tribute of *The Magic Presence,* King states:

"The hour is at hand when the humanity of this Earth must give more recognition to the Activity of the Great Ascended Masters and Angelic Host, who are constantly pouring out Their Transcendent Light and Assistance to mankind. There must come more conscious cooperation between the outer physical life of humanity and these Great Beings who are the Protectors and Teachers of the human beings in this World." [47]

Angels, Gabriel told us, attend every meeting of world leaders and do their best to influence them in positive directions. But, of course, all humans have free choice which angels cannot override.

There is some conjecture as to whether Abraham Lincoln received instructions to free the slave population. Perhaps he did.

"It remains a subject of argument between historians and Spiritualists as to the extent to which Lincoln was influenced by spirit guidance in his decision to free the slaves. Certainly at the start of the Civil War it had not been his intention to end slavery in the South." [48]

Gabriel told us that Woodrow Wilson received the idea of League of Nations from spirit. Even more startling, Gabriel explained that FDR had also been advised by spirit. Pres. Roosevelt listed to some of it, but not all of the guidance. *If he had followed all of it there would not have been a second world war.* This hit me to the core, for I was a young teenager during WWII, and recalled too vividly the horror of it, including the loss of my brother Blake, who gave his life in Europe.

Spirit Instruction

Gen. 24:27

And he said, Blessed be the Lord God of my master Abraham, who hath not left destitute my master of his mercy and his truth: I being in the way, the Lord led me to the house of my master's brethren.

Acts 2:1-4

And when the day of Pentecost was fully come, they were all with one accord in one place.

And suddenly there came a sound from heaven as of a rushing mighty wind, and it filled all the house where they were sitting..

And there appeared unto them cloven tongues like as of a fire, and it sat upon each of them.

And they were all filled with the Holy Ghost, and began to speak with other tongues, as the Spirit gave them utterance.

Swedenborg

"In 1745, at the age of fifty-seven, Swedenborg had an experience that radically changed the course of is life. Much later, he would describe it as a vision of Jesus Christ commissioning him to 'open to people the spiritual meaning of Scripture' and initiating years of regular experiences of the spiritual world. Soon after this vision, he resigned from his post on the Swedish Board of Mines and spent the remainder of his years writing and publishing the theological works which he is now best known." [49]

Cayce

Cayce relates his first vision at age fourteen:

> "Kneeling by my bed that night, I prayed again that God would show me that He loved me, that He would give me the ability to do something for my fellow man which would show to them His love, even as the actions of His little creatures in the woods showed me their trust in one who loved them. . . .I was not yet asleep when the vision first began . . . A glorious light as of the rising morning sun seemed to fill the whole room, and a figure appeared at the foot of my bed. . . . an angel, or what, I knew not; but gently, patiently, it said, 'Thy prayers are heard. You will have you wish.

120

Remain faithful. Be true to yourself. Help the sick, the afflicted." [50]

Prophecy

The Persian Sibyl: "When the time predicted shall come in which the Redeemer is to come into the world, the sound of a voice will be heard in the deserts, and that voice will invite mortals to prepare the way and cleanse their souls of vices and sins, and they will be baptized in pure and limpid waters". [51]

Sibyls
". . . The Erythraean Sibyl, which foretold the coming of Christ, and his sufferings. His words are: 'He will fall into the hostile hands of the wicked; with poisonous spittle will they spit upon him; on the sacred back they will strike him; they will crown him with a crown of thorns; they will give him gall for food, and vinegar for drink. The veil of the temple will be rent, and at midday there will be darkness of three hours long. And he will die, repose three days in sleep, and then, in the joyful light, he will come again as a first'." [52]

Oracles
A story about testing the oracles is told by Herodotus, according to *Herodotus I: 21-25*:
"Croesus, King of Lydia, wished to make war on Cyrus, but feared to do so without the express sanction of Heaven. This was to be learned, of course, through the oracles. But it was first necessary to test the veracity of these. Accordingly, he dispatched envoys to six of the best known oracles then existing: those of Delphi, Dodona, Branchidae, Zeus Ammon, Trophonius, and Amphiaraus. On the hundredth day from their departure, the envoys were to ask these several oracles what was Croesus doing at home in Sardis at a *particular moment*. He had carefully kept the

secret to himself, and had chosen an action which was beyond all possible conjecture.

"Four oracles failed; Amphiaraus was nearly right. Delphi alone   succeeded perfectly. This was the response, as given by Herodotus:

'I can count the sands, and I can measure the Ocean;

I have ears for the silent, and know what the dumb man meaneth;

Lo! On my sense there striketh the smell of a shell-covered tortoise,

Boiling now on a fire, with the flesh of a lamb, in a cauldron, ---

Brass in the vessel below, and brass the cover above it.' [53]

Scripture

Hundreds of years prior to Jesus' birth, Isaiah prophesies:

Isaiah. 9:6

For unto us a child is born, unto us a son is given: and the government shall be upon his shoulder: and his name shall be called Wonderful, Counsellor, The mighty God, The everlasting Father, The Prince of Peace

Exodus 15:21

And Miriam answered them, Sing ye to the Lord, for he hath triumphed gloriously; the horse and his rider hath he thrown into the sea.

Judges 4:7

And I will draw unto thee to the river Keshon Sisera, the captain of Jabin's army, with his chariots and his multitude; and I will deliver him unto thine hand.

Matthew 8:17

That it might be fulfilled which was spoken by Esaias the prophet, saying, Himself took our infirmities, and bare our sicknesses.

John 4:21

Jesus saith unto her, Woman, believe me, the hour cometh, when ye shall neither in this mountain, nor yet at Jerusalem, worship the Father.

I Corinthians 14:22

Wherefore tongues are for a sign, not to them that believe, but to them that believe not: but prophesying serveth not for them that believe not, but for them which believe.

Constantine

"Perhaps the most famous prophetic dream in history was that bestowed upon Constantine in 312 as he prepared to invade Rome and claim the throne of Emperor Maxentius. The night before the great battle and angel appeared in Constantine's dreams bearing the Chi-Rho monogram of Christ. 'By this conquer,' directed the angel. Accordingly, Constantine's men went into combat with the emblem on their shields, and Maxentius obligingly made the dumbest military move of his life (never fight with your back to a river). Thunderstruck, Constantine called his advisers together and inquired which god was represented by the sign. Finding that it was the symbol of Christ, Constantine promptly converted, and with him, Europe." [54]

St.Malachi

"In the year 1139 [Malachi] undertook a journey to Rome to visit Pope Innocent III, and on the way . . . he wrote down his famous prophecy concerning the popes." [55]

Nostradamus

One of the Nostradamus stanzas runs like this:
"The young lion will conquer the old one upon the field in single combat. He will pierce his eyes in a golden cage, who will then die a dreadful death." The manifestation of this prophecy is herewith explained:

Nostradamus was a contemporary of King Henry II of France. In July 1559, King Henry celebrated the marriage of his sister . . . as part of the festivities held a magnificent tournament . . . invited one of his guests, the young Earl of Montgomery, of the Scots Guard, to cross lances with him in the tourney. The young north Briton modestly declined this too great and too dangerous honor. The King, however, insisted, and in the heat of the tilting the Earl's lance pierced the golden visor of his opponent's helmet, entered his right eye, and Henry II died soon thereafter a horribly painful death." [56]

Swedenborg

Swedenborg also predicted the Russian emperor's death:
"In the year 1762, on the very day when Peter III of Russian died,
Swedenborg . . . said, "Now, at this very hour, the Emperor Peter III
has died in prison --- explaining the nature of his death . . . The papers
soon after announced the death of the Emperor, which had taken place
on the very same day." [57]

Andew Jackson Davis

Davis was born in 1826 in New York State; a born clairvoyant. . . He
wrote a five volume work entitled *The Great Harmonia.* It described his
many visions. Davis "foresaw not only the ultimate spiritualization of
America, but that this spiritualization would come about in virtue of
leisure owing to numerous mechanical and labor-saving devices, many
of which he foresaw with a quite remarkable lucidity." [58]

CHAPTER 12
PHYSICAL MEDIUMSHIP

Fire Mediumship

Exod 3:2
And the angel of the Lord appeared unto him in a flame of fire out of the midst of a bush: and he looked, and, behold, the bush burned with fire, and the bush was not consumed.

Dan. 3:25
He answered and said, Lo, I see four men loose, walking in the midst of the fire, and they have no hurt; and the form of the fourth is like the Son of God.

John 21:9
As soon as they were come to land, they saw a fire of coals there, and fish laid thereon, and bread.

B. T. Spaulding
One of the members of the Himalayan expedition described walking through flames:

> "The lightning ignited the grass . . . and before we
> knew it, we were virtually surrounded by a forest fire. . .
> [the guides] said 'There are two ways of escape.
> One is to try to get to the next creek, where there is
> water flowing through a deep canyon . . . about five
> miles away . . . the other way is to go on through the
> fire with us if you can trust us to take you through.'
>
> "Throwing myself . . . wholly upon their protection, I
> stepped between them and we proceeded on our way,
> which seemed to be in the direction the fire was raging
> the most. Then immediately it seemed as if a great
> archway opened before us and we went on directly
> through that fire, without the least inconvenience,
> either from smoke or heat. . there were at least six miles
> of this fire-swept area that we passed through. . . until

we crossed a small stream and then were out of the fire" [1]

Healing

Gen. 20:17

So Abraham prayed unto God: and God healed Abimelech, and his wife, and his maidservants; and they bore children.

Lev.1:18

The flesh also, in which even in the skin thereof, was a boil, and is healed,

Ps. 30:2

O Lord my God, I cried unto thee, and thou hast healed me.

Mark 2:11-12

I say unto thee, Arise, and take up thy bed, and go thy way into thine house.
And immediately he arose, took up the bed, and went forth before them all; insomuch that they were all amazed, and glorified God, saying, We never saw it on this fashion.

Luke 17:14

And when he saw them, he said unto them, Go show yourselves unto the priests. And it came to pass, that, as they went, they were cleansed.

John 5:8-9

Jesus saith unto him, Rise, take up thy bed, and walk.
And immediately the man was made whole, and took up his bed, and walked: and on the same day was the sabbath.

Acts 8:7

For unclean spirits, crying with loud voice, came out of many that were possessed of them: and many were taken with palsies, and that were lame, were healed.

Cayce

Among the 15,000 readings given by Edgar Cayce over a period of 40 years; 8,976 were devoted to medical issues. In a trance state he healed thousands, many of whom lived miles away. Given the name and

126

location of an ailing individual, he identified the physical ailment and advised proper treatment.

Faith Healing

From *The Edgar Cayce Primer:*

There are several stories in the Bible about Jesus' healings, after which he tells the person 'thy faith has made thee whole.' One of them follows:

Matt 9:22
But Jesus turned him about, and when he saw her, he said, Daughter, be of good comfort; thy faith hath made thee whole. And the woman was made whole from that hour.

Myrtle Fillmore
"By the spring of 1886, it appeared that the end of life for Myrtle Fillmore was near. . . . In a dream she heard voices calling to her and she saw hands beckoning to her, apparently from another realm of existence. But she felt a strong force on this earth plane holding her in the visible realm. Shortly after this . . . Dr. E.B.Weeks from the Illinois Metaphysical College came to Kansas City [to lecture]. As she left his lecture that night, one sentence illumined the very depths of her soul:
'I am a child of God and therefore I do no inherit sickness.' . . .
"She took within her this new Truth she had learned, and she talked to her body. . . She closed herself in a room . . . studied the Four Gospels.
She sat next to an empty chair and she *knew* that the Spirit of Jesus Christ occupied that chair and was supporting her and encouraging her in her quest. . . she was healed completely, about 1888. Of her healing she said, *'The truth came to me – a great revelation, showing me that I am a child of the one whole and perfect mind, created to express the health that God is.'*[2]

Burn doctors

A *Foxfire Book* of 1972 (pp. 349-368) reported on faith healers in the southern Appalachian Mountains. They were known as 'burn doctors', because they could 'blow out' burns and prevent blisters. They could also heal thrush and bleeding. Some medical doctors accepted their ability.

Burns - A woman known as Aunt Nora Garland said the way she healed burns was to "pass her hand over the burn three times, blow her breath gently over it following the hand each time, and repeat the (Bible) verse silently each time." She must be present to draw fire. She did not have to be present to stop bleeding.

Another woman gave the 'secret phrase' on the condition that she not be named. When asked why she would do that, she said, "Well, it might be of some use to you when I'm gone. I believe in th' healin' power because the Lord has healed me. I know He has. That's the greatest thing they is, is th' healin' power of th' Savior." This is the verse, unedited, that she provided:

> Thair came an angel
> From the East bringing
> frost and fire. In frost out
> fire. In the name of
> the father the Son and
> of the Holy Goost

Thrush - Charley Tyler could heal thrush. Holding the child in his arms he would get the infant to laugh or cry, and then cupping his fingers around the child's mouth he would suck the air from the baby – not blow into its mouth – and then blow the air away from the child . He would do that three times, and the thrush was gone. In a severe case he would have to do it twice.

Bleeding - Aunt Nora Garland said she did not have to be with the patient or know anything about them, even their name. "You just think about 'em and say th' verse three times."

Paul Gunn

"On October 27, 1949, Paul Gunn attended a religious service conduced by Kathryn Kuhlman in the auditorium of the Carnegie Library, Pittsburgh, Pennsylvania. He had advanced cancer of the left lung, walked with difficulty with the help of two canes, and was in great pain. He was booked into the city's Presbyterian Hospital for surgery two days later to remove the lung . . . He describes what happened in his own words: 'Suddenly the power of God came down. It hit me and just for an instant the sensation of burning fire in my lung was more intense than it had ever been before. I thought I couldn't stand it . . .And then, it was all over --- just like that. . . . Two days after the service, Gunn . . was thoroughly examined, and . . . tested. . . Records show that he was at the same job 12 years later, and had not missed a single day due to illness since his cure." [3] (from *I Believe in Miracles*, by Kuhlman)

Psychic Surgery
"In his book, *The Romeo Error* (1976), the celebrated biologist and researcher Lyall Watson gives a detailed account of one of over a thousand Filipino psychic operations that he has witnessed. . . [He] concluded with the statement: 'Something very extraordinary still happens in the Philippines.'" [4]

Healing of Magnetized Articles

II Kings 5:34
And he went up, and lay upon the child, and put his mouth upon his mouth, and his eyes upon his eyes, and his hands upon his hands: and he stretched himself upon the child; and the flesh of the child waxed warm.

Matt. 14:36
And besought him that they might only touch the hem of his garment: and as many as touched were made perfectly whole.

Acts 19:11-12
And God wrought special miracles by the hands of Paul:

129

*So that from his body were brought unto the sick handkerchiefs or aprons, and the
diseases departed from them, and the evil spirits went out of them.*

Apocrypha
First Gospel of the Infancy of Jesus Christ, IX: 4-5
*St. Mary hearing her, said, Take a little of that water with which I have washed
my son, and sprinkle it upon him.*
*Then she took a little of that water, as St. Mary had commanded, and sprinkled I
upon her son, who being wearied with his violent pains, had fallen asleep; and after
he had slept a little, awaked perfectly well and recovered.*

*To this Mary agreed, and when the mother of Caleb was gone, she made a coat for
her son of the swaddling cloth, put it on him, and his disease was cured;* X:3

*And when she had placed him in the bed wherein Christ lay, at the moment when
his eyes were just closed by death; as soon as ever the smell of the garments of the
Lord Jesus Christ reached the boy, his eyes were opened, and calling with a loud
voice to his mother he asked for bread . . . XI:6*

*Again there was a leprous woman who went to the Lady St. Mary, the mother of
Jesus, and said, O my Lady, help me . . .*
*St. Mary replied to her, Wait a little till I have washed my son Jesus, and put him
to bed.*
*The woman waited, as she was commanded; and Mary when she had put Jesus in
bed, giving her the water with which she had washed his body, said, Take some of
the water, and pour it upon thy body;*
*Which when she had done, she instantly became clean, and praised God, and gave
thanks to him. XII:1-6*

Materialization

Gen. 19:1
*And there came two angels to Sodom at even; and Lot sat in the gate of Sodom:
and Lot seeing them rose up to meet them; and he bowed himself with his face
toward the ground;*

Matt 28:9

And as they went to tell his disciples, behold, Jesus met them, saying, all hail. And they came and held him by the feet, and worshipped him.

Native Americans

According to the Lakota, the *heyoka* are those who have seen the Thunderbird in a vision, and because of this they are able to reach into boiling water with bare hands to take out pieces of boiled dog meat during the *heyoka* ceremony; they are able to predict stormy weather, and in some cases to control it.

The Shawnee Prophet

> On a spring night in 1805, living in Indiana as a sickly member of Tecumseh's band, Lalawethika fell into a trance and experienced a divine revelation that changed the course of his life. Like Handsome Lake and a number of other visionaries and prophets who appeared at the time among the disheartened Indian nations, Lalawethika reported tht he had gone to the spirit world and seen the Creator, who had told him to change his bad ways and become a teacher who could carry the Creator's messages to the people and lead them along the right path. . . Taking the new, more appropriate name Tenskwatawa, meaning 'Open Door,' he began to preach to the Shawnee . . ." [5]

Abraham Lincoln

Sometimes those in spirit choose to reveal themselves in a photo taken after their death. Mary Todd Lincoln, as a widow, appeared for a formal photo incognito (veiled in mourning). When the print was taken, the photographer recognized an apparition standing behind Mrs. Lincoln as the late president. "Mary Lincoln agreed, and added, 'I am his widow'." [6]

Another story about Abraham Lincoln. "In a dream of his own dath, Abraham Lincoln stood at the foot of a coffin in the White House and saw a shrouded corpse. When he asked who had died, a soldier among the shadowy mourners answered: "The President. He was killed by an assassin." [7]

Beholding The Master Jesus in person
"As I looked about at the beauty, I became aware of a figure coming toward me. He looked vaguely familiar, dressed in his long white robe. He had beautiful auburn hair, and a rich reddish beard. But it was smile, his dancing, glowing eyes, his radiating joy, that just took my breath away . . .'You're Jesus?' I asked. He just smiled bigger and again, just nodded his head up and down." [8]

The author had a glorious experience in March of 1984, during my first séance. Shortly after the circle commenced, I saw the Master standing about 8 feet in front of me. His brilliant blue eyes held my gaze. His hair was auburn with reddish highlights. His arms were outstretched toward me and on his upturned hands was a huge loaf of bread. He said to me, "Lay down your life for me, and I will give you the bread of life". I did not understand his words at that time, but as the ensuing weeks unfolded I stopped my addiction to alcohol. Then it became clear to me that if I surrendered to his guidance I could be blessed by him with an enduring sobriety. And I know now that Jesus *always* keeps his promise.

Ministering of Angels

Gen. 19:15
   And when the morning arose, then the angels hastened Lot, saying, Arise, take thy wife, and thy two daughters, which are here; lest thou be consumed in the iniquity of the city.

Joshua 5:13-14
   And it came to pass, when Joshua was by Jericho, that he lifted up his eyes and looked, and, behold, there stood a man over against him whit his sword drawn in his hand: and Joshua went unto him, and said unto him, Art thou for us, or for our adversaries?
   And he said, Nay; but as captain of the host of the Lord am I now come. And Joshua fell on his face to the earth, and did worship, and said unto him, What saith my lord unto his servant?

Psalm 91:10-12
   There shall no evil befall thee, neither shall any plague come nigh thy dwelling. For he shall give his angels charge over thee, to keep thee in all thy ways.

Matt. 26:53

Thinkest thou that I cannot now pray to my Father, and he shall presently give me more than twelve legions of angels?

Luke 4:10-11

For it is written, He shall give his angels charge over thee, to keep thee: And in their hands they shall bear thee up, lest at any time thou dash thy foot against a stone.

Acts 8:26

And the angel of the Lord spake unto Philip, saying, Arise, and go toward the south unto the way that goeth down from Jerusalem unto Gaza, which is desert.

I believe that the divine intervention of angels occurs much more than we realize. But there are times when it is blatantly evident, as when an unseen helper saved a child from drowning in the bathtub:

Kathleen McConnell

Mrs. McConnell and her family moved into an historic home in St. Louis, only to find that the house was already inhabited by three young, unseen children. She named them and researched the history of the house. Eventually they left to return to Heaven. Here is one amazing story she tells of in her book *Don't Call Them Ghosts*. After leaving two children in the bathtub, the older watching the younger, Mrs. McConnell reports:

> "As I walked just a few steps down the hall, I felt some uneasiness . . . It was too quiet . . . I stood over the tub. [the older child had left the tub unbeknownst to Mrs. McConnell] My baby had evidently pulled himself up by the faucet handles only to turn the water on full force . . . I was surprised he wasn't sliding down the sloped end. He was laughing and grinning . . . even though both faucets were on, the water was not hot at all . . . As the water drained I could see Duncan wasn't sitting or even standing in the tub . . . Something . . . held him suspended above the surface of the rushing water. Neither his little butt nor his feet were touching the bottom of the tub. He was being held against the

contour of the back of the tub. . . I was spellbound . . .
Whoever was holding him up held fast to their grip
until all the water was gone from the tub. All I could do
was lean back on the heels of my feet and watch in
amazement as he was finally lowered back down to a
sitting position in the tub. . . He could have drowned .
. . He was perfectly safe in the hands of his unseen
guardian. [9]

K. Malarkey
Divine intervention at an auto accident was described by a boy,
observing angels rescue his father from the vehicle:

"Five angels were carrying Daddy outside the car. Four were carrying
his body, and one was supporting his neck and head. The angels were
big and muscular, like wrestlers, and they had wings on their backs
from their waists to their shoulders." [10]

The strangest part of this story, I believe, is that when conversing with
angels Alex and the angels spoke in a different language. The different
language was not explained, but obviously Alex understood it, and
spoke it.

"He continued speaking in his 'Heaven language,' as Aaron had called
it, and then he fell silent. After a moment, Alex's normal voice asked us
to pull back the sheet.
'It was an angel,' Alex said. 'He came here to comfort me. He touched
my head.'" [11]

In the Finger Lakes region of New York State one of the dangers when
driving is hitting a deer at high speed. At my request, my daughter,
Evie, wrote down her experience with hitting a deer when she was
homeward bound, in 1997.

It was mid-September and I'd been at my new teaching
job, 53 miles from home, for about three weeks.
Thursdays were laundry days in Canandaigua, and this
was a Thursday evening . . . I was finally on my way
home . . . It was just dusk but still light enough to see

the deer jump in front of me just two miles from home. I slammed on the brakes, locking them, and hit the deer broadside.

"I remember seeing the deer's four hooves perfectly suspended at my eye level, through the windshield. I also remember the circular spin the car went into - when moments turn into an eternity - and holding the steering wheel for dear life.

And then, pure calm, with the sensation of being enveloped by huge wings of love. I was no longer in control of the car, its path, or my life.
When I opened my eyes, the first thought in my head was 'get home'.
The thought repeated itself until it manifested . . . in words when I repeated them out loud. My car was running! I looked [to see that] . . .I was on a driveway with tree-top leaves in front of me. 'Get home' came again and again.
My car was facing north; I'd been driving south. I drove through the leaves to the main road. I drove home but could not get out of the car; now it was dark.
I clamored over the gear shift and got out of the passenger door. I called my daughter's Dad, my voice quaking. I would not be able to tell you what was said but he was . . . there within an hour.

The damages: There was glass in my shoes, glass in my purse, glass throughout the laundry basket, glass in all four foot wells. Every window in the car was broken or blown out. The driver's door was caved in far enough to be jammed closed. The next day my car was deemed 'totaled' . . . My only injury was a tiny scratch at the base of my left pinky finger – the one closest to the driver's door – without a trace of blood.

The following day I went to the site of the accident. The deer was dead on the East side of the road. On the West side of the road, where Canandaigua Lake is far below the 'high banks' of Bare Hill, three cement guard posts were broken off and five sapling trees cut off at their base, but the most amazing part was that my car had come to rest on a driveway 15 feet down from the main road. I slowly drove my rental car down the driveway and saw the trees I'd driven through the night before, tree tops and entire trees. But the strangest thing of all [was that] pieces of my laundry, which had flown out of the shattered windows, scattered among tree limbs that my car had never touched.

It had been a miracle. I was protected by love.

Physical Phenomena

APPORTS

Ex 15:19
For the horse of Pharaoh went in with his chariots and with his horsemen into the sea, and the Lord brought again the waters of the sea upon them; but the children of Israel went on dry land in the midst of the sea.

II Kings 6:6
And the man of God said, Where fell it? And he shewed him the place. And he cut down a stick, and cast it in thither; and the iron did swim.

John 21:6
And he said unto them, Cast the net on the right side of the ship, and ye shall find. They cast therefore, and now they were not able to draw it for the multitude of fishes.

Swedenborg
"It may therefore be stated in advance that of the Lord's Divine mercy it has been granted me now for some years to he constantly and uninterruptedly in company with spirits and angels, hearing them speak and in turn speaking with them. [12]

Spaulding

From *Life and Teaching of the Masters of the Far East*, a member of an expedition to the Himalayas reports what he saw from the banks of a raging river:

> ". . . the twelve, fully dressed, walked to the bank of the stream, and with the utmost composure stepped on the water, not into it. I never shall forget my feelings as I saw each of those twelve men step from solid ground upon the running water . . . so astonished were we to see those twelve men walking calmly across the surface of the stream without the least inconvenience and not sinking below the soles of their sandals. When they stepped from the water to the farther bank I felt that tons of weight had been lifted off my shoulders, and I believe this was the feeling of every one of our party, judging from the sighs of relief as the last man stepped ashore." [13]

Steiger
Having previously suffered from rheumatic fever and having a NDE, Sherry had seen angels before. Later, an angel visited her: When eight years old, at a summer camp in Michigan, Sherry had an angel manifest to her and her friends:

"The angelic being appeared to come down through the ceiling of the cabin in which Sherry was staying, and most of the startled girls went down on their knees and folded their hands in prayer." [14]

"I overdosed on cocaine and knew I was dying . . . With time running out, I begged repeatedly to live, to stay in this world. . . . My body dematerialized as it was lifted to another place. The images I paint now are echoes of this experience." [15]

Lakota
According to the Lakota, the *heyoka* are those who have seen the Thunderbird in a vision, and because of this they are able to reach into boiling water with bare hands to take out pieces of boiled dog meat during the *heyoka* ceremony; they are able to predict stormy weather, and in some cases to control it.

Sir William Barrett

"Sir William Barrett was a witness at one of the Goligher séances. He described later how he had seen the table suspended 18 inches in the air with no one touching it. He was unable to press the table down, using all his strength. When he climbed onto it to force it down, he was promptly thrown off. After this the table turned upside down on the floor. He was asked to lift it up, but was unable to move it. It "appeared screwed down to the floor,' he attested." [16]

"Materializations are not usual in séances today, but they still occur. But, Silver Belle, a spirit manifested by the medium Ethel Post-Parrish, of Ephrata, Pennsylvania, was photographed in 1953." [17]

K. Malarkey
From *The Boy Who Came Back from Heaven:*
Page 14: ". . . Five angels were carrying Daddy outside the car. Four were carrying his body and one was supporting his neck and head. . ."

Also, a description of angels:
"They [angels] are completely white and have wings. . ." [18]

After holy visits from angels, his face revealed a change in its appearance.

"The angels have visited me many times . . . People have told me that after I am with the angels my face is glowing – like a thousand Christmas mornings. . ." [19]

Spirit Levitation

I Kings 18:12
And it shall come to pass, as soon as I am gone from thee, that the Spirit of the Lord shall carry thee whither I know not; and so when I come and tell Ahab, and he cannot find thee, he shall slay me: but I thy servant fear the Lord from my youth.

Ezek. 3:12
Then the spirit took me up, and I heard behind me a voice of a great rushing, saying, Blessed be the glory of the Lord from this place.

Mark 16:19

So then after the Lord had spoken unto them, he was received up into heaven, and sat on the right hand of God.

Luke 24:51

And it came to pass, while he blessed them, he was parted from them, and carried up into heaven.

Acts 5:19-20

But the angel of the Lord by night opened the prison doors, and brought them forth, and said,

Go, stand and speak in the temple to the people all the words of this life.

Acts 8:39

And when they were come up out of the water, the Spirit of the Lord caught away Philip, that the eunuch saw him no more: and he went on his way rejoicing.

Sir William Crookes

Sir William Crookes, of England, photographed Katie King, spirit control of medium Florence Cook. [20]

Dr. Alfred Russell Wallace

Dr. Alfred Russell Wallace, British naturalist, held séances in his own home. In séances with Mrs. Guppy, levitation was a common occurrence.

"An even more astonishing aspect of her power was the ability to make delicate flowers and other objects materialize out of the thin air." (This is known as apports). [21]

Spirit Lights

Gen. 15:17

And it came to pass, that, when the sun went down, and it was dark, behold a smoking furnace, and a burning lamp that passed between those pieces.

Exod. 13:21-22

And he Lord went before them by day in a pillar of a cloud, to lead them the way; and by night in a pillar of fire, to give them light; to go by day and night.

He took not away the pillar of the cloud by day, nor the pillar of the fire by night, from before the people.

Exod. 34:29-30

And it came to pass, when Moses came down from mount Sinai with the two tables of testimony in Moses' hand, when he came down from the mount, that Moses wist not that the skin of his face shone while he talked with him.

And when Aaron and all the children of Israel saw Moses, behold, the skin of his face shone; and they were afraid to come nigh him.

Sherman
"The dead are alive and they try to prove it in many ways. One way they show this is by talking to us through our tape recorders . . . . Recently, one of my daughters had a serious auto accident. She told me the following morning that shortly before the accident she had a strong impression she should not continue on the highway. At the same time there was a purple light around the steering wheel . . . ignoring both . . .she continued on her way. A short time later the accident occurred. When I went to my tape recorder later that morning and asked what the purple light was that my daughter had seen, I was told, 'Mom Wilson was there'.[Mom Wilson had died 3 years earlier]." [22]

The wisdom of spirit is available to all, and Gabriel told us that there are many, many entities in the spirit world who are waiting for someone on earth to accept their teachings. As we each turn within and understand that the spirit world of God exists, we can then open our minds to receiving desired information, guidance, instruction and even messages for others, as we desire.

The Light of Truth
"If the reader will trust to his own indwelling Spirit of truth for light, he will find in these suggestions a guide to endless inspiration in the understanding of Truth. . . We are always pleased when any one learns to go within and get his inspiration direct from his own indwelling Lord or Spirit of truth." [23]

140

Appendix A
Psychic Phenomena in Scripture

OLD TESTAMENT

Genesis
Clairvoyance – 15:1
Spirit communication in Dreams – 28:12
         31:11-13
         31:24
         37:5-10
         41:1-5
Trance – 15:12-15
Fire Mediumship – 19:24
Physical Phenomena – 24:15
      15:17
      32:24-30
Spirit Lights – 3:24
    15:17
Independent Spirit Voice – 3:8-24
       6:3
       21:17
       22:11
       22:15
       46:2-4
Materialization – 18:1-10
     19:1
     32:24
Apports – 14:18
Ministering of Angels – 21:17-20
        32:1-2
Counseling - 44:5
    44:15
Spirit Instruction – 24:7

Exodus
Fire Mediumship – 3:2
      14:24-25

Independent Spirit Voice – 3:14-21
6:10-11
Physical Phenomena – 3:-20
4:2-9
6:1-8
7:1-5
7:8-9
7: 10, 12
7:14-19
7:20-21
8:9-13
Chapters 16,17, 19-21, 23-25, 26-31, 40

Spirit Lights – 3:2
34:29
Prophecy – 15:21
Inspirational Trance - 4:12
4:14-16

Independent spirit voice – 4:2-4
19:1-6
34:1
Independent Spirit Writing - 24:12
31:18
32: 15-16
34:1
Materialization – 24:10
Ministering of Angels – 3:5
Counseling – 4:17
Spirit Instruction – 4:14-27

Leviticus 0

Numbers
Trance – 24:4
Healing – 21:8-9
Apports – 11:31 (quails)
17:8 (budding almonds)
Independent Spirit Voice – 11:25

Deuteronomy
Independent Spirit Writing – 9:10
Independent Spirit Voice – 5:6-21

Joshua
Ministering of Angels – 5:13-15

Judges
Fire Mediumship – 15:14
Physical Phenomena – 6:37-40
Materialization – 13:3
Ministering of Angels – 2:1-3
                                     15:14
Prophecy – 4:1-7
Spirit Instruction – 6:40
                             14:19

Ruth (0)

I Samuel
Clairvoyance – 9:6
Prophetic Reading – 10:6
Trance – 10:6-8
Seances Recorded – chapter 28 (Endor)
Séance – music – 16:23
Independent Spirit Voice – 3:3-14
                                     9:17
Materialization – 28:12-19
Spirit Guidance – 3:1-21
Counseling – 9:3-27
                        28:7-19

II Samuel (0)

I Kings
Fire Mediumship – 19:6
Physical Phenomena – 19:6-7
                                19:11-12
Spirit Levitation – 18:12
Healing – 17:17-24
Independent Spirit Voice – 19:5-13
Apports – 19:6

II Kings
Clairvoyance – 6:12-17
Séance – music – 3:15
Spirit Levitation – 6:5-6

Healing – 4:32-37 (boy child)
          5:1-14 (Naaman)
Healing of magnetized articles – 4:29-30

I Chronicles (0)

II Chronicles
Independent Spirit Writing – 21:12

Ezra (0), Nehemiah (0), Esther (0)

Job
Spirit Communication in Dreams – 4:15-21
                                33:15-33
Psalms
Apports – 78:24-28 (manna)
Ministering of Angels – **Chapter** 91

Proverbs (0), Ecclesiastes (0), Song of Solomon (0)

Isaiah
Prophecy 9:6 (Jesus' birth, function, titles)

Jeremiah (2)
Clairvoyance – 1:11
               1:13
Lamentations (0)

Ezekiel – entire book prophecy/trance
Physical Phenomena – 8:3
Spirit Levitation – 3:12-14
                    8:3
                    11:1
Independent Spirit Voice – 1:24
                           1:25
                           1:28
                           4:1-17
Spirit Lights – 1:14
Materialization - **Chapter 1**
                  2:9-10
Prophecy - 11:9
Apports – 2:9-10

Counseling – **Chapter 14**

Daniel
Spirit Communication in Dreams – 2:19-45
(Daniel/night vision)   8:18
                                        10:9
Fire Mediumship – 3:25
Independent Spirit Writing – 5:5
Materialization – 5:5
                    3:22-25
Spirit Guidance – 6:22
Counseling – 2:19-45

Hosea (0)

Joel
Spirit Communication in Dreams – 2:28
Promise of Continuance of Spirit Power – 2:28

**Amos, Obadiah, Jonah, Micah, Nahum,
Habakkuk, Zephaniah, Haggai, Zechariah,
Malachi – (O)**

NEW TESTAMENT

Matthew
Spirit Communication in Dreams – 27:19

Physical Phenomena – 28:2
Ministering of Angels – 26:53
Matrialization - 28:9
Prophecy – 2:5-6
                    2:17
                    2:23
                    4:14
                    8:17
                    13:14
                    13:35
                    15:7
                    21:5
                    21:13

Mark
Inspirational Speaking – 13:11
Healing – 3:2-5
Ministering of Angels -16:20

Luke
Healing - 5:17-25
            9:11
            14:2-4
            17:12-14
Spiritual Gifts of Healing – 9:2
                            10:9
Materialization – 1:11-20
                  1:26-35
                  2:9-14
                  2:27

Ministering of Angels – 4:10-11
Prophecy – 1:67-79

John
Clairvoyance – 4:18
Prophecy – 4:21-23
Fire Mediumship – 21:9
Physical Phenomena – 20:30
                          21:6-11
Healing – 5:8-9
Independent Spirit Voice – 12:28-30
Materialization – 20:12-17 Jesus/Easter
                  20:19-29
                  21:4
                  21:14
Apports – 21:9
          21:13
Ministering of Angels – 14:26
                        15:26

Acts
Materialization – 16:9
Independent Spirit Voice – 16:9
Trance – 9:3-9
          10:10

Spirit Communication in Dreams – 9:10-12
                                 16:9
Speaking in Tongues – 2:4
Physical Phenomena – 2:2
                    5:19
                    12:7-10
Inspirational Speaking – 2:4
Spirit Levitation – 5:19
                8:39
Healing - 3:1-8
        5:15-16
        8:6-7
        9:18
        14:8-10
        16:16-18
        28:-8-9
Healing of magnetized articles – 19:11-12
Independent Spirit Voice – 7:30-34
                        9:4-6
                        9:10-12
                        9:15-16
Materialization – 1:10-11
Apports – 5:19
        5:23
        16:9
Ministering of Angels – 4:31
                    5:18-19
                    6:5
                    7:35
                    8:26-29
                    9:1-7
                    9:10-16
                    12:7
                    21:4
Prophecy – 2:18
        21:10
Spirit Guidance – 11:12-15
Counseling – 5:3-6
            5:9-10
            9:17
Spirit Instruction – 2:1-19

Romans – (0)

147

I Corinthians
Speaking in Tongues – 14:18-23
Spiritual Gifts – 12: 1-11
12:28-31
Prophecy – 12:28
14:22-24

II Corinthians
Trance – 12:2-4
Independent Spirit Voice – 12:4

Galatians
Spirit Guidance – 2:1-2

**Ephesians, Philippians, Colossians,
Thessalonians, Timothy, Titus, Philemon –
(0)**

Hebrews
Ministering of Angels – 1:1-13
2:2-9
James, Peter, John, Jude –(0)

**The Revelation of St. John the Divine
Entire book includes several examples
psychic phenomena, including
Independent Spirit Voice, Ministering of
Angels, Visions, Prophecy, Materialization,
and Spirit Instruction**

Apocrypha
The Apocrypha contains many examples of
several kinds of psychic phenomena. Some are
included in the text. It is suggested the reader
seek them in the apocryphal books.

Appendix B – NSAC Principles

Declaration of Principles of the National Spiritualism Association of Churches.

1. We believe in Infinite Intelligence.
2. We believe that the phenomena of Nature, both physical and spiritual, are the expression of Infinite Intelligence.
3. We affirm that a correct understanding of such expression and living in accordance therewith, constitute true religion.
4. We affirm that the existence and personal identity of the individual continue after the change called death.
5. We affirm that communication with the so-called dead is a fact, scientifically proven by the phenomena of Spiritualism.
6. We believe that the highest morality is contained in the Golden Rule: "Do unto others as you would have them do unto you."
7. We affirm the moral responsibility of individuals, and that we make our own happiness or unhappiness as we obey or disobey Nature's physical and spiritual laws.
8. We affirm that the doorway to reformation is never closed against any soul here or hereafter.
9. We affirm that the precepts of Prophecy and Healing are Divine attributes proven through Mediumship.

Appendix C
Divination methods and their primary focus

Aeromancy – clouds, winds etc.
Alectryomancy - roosters
Aleuromancy – flour
Alomancy – salt
Alphitomancy – wheat or barley
Amniomancy - birth caul
Astragalomancy – knuckle bones
Austromancy – wind
Axinomancy – axe
Belomancy – arrows
Bibliomancy – book
Botanomancy – plants
Capnomancy – smoke
Catoptromancy – mirrors
Cartomancy – playing cards/tarot
Causmomancy – fire
Cephalomancy – donkey skull
Ceraunoscopy – wind
Ceroscopy – molten wax
Cheiromancy – palmistry
Cleidomancy – key on a thread
Cleromancy – dice (casting of lots)
Coscinomancy – sieve and tongs
Critomancy – food
Cromniomancy – onions
Crystallomancy – crystal gazing
Cyclomancy – (wheel of fortune)
Dactylomancy – rings
Daphnomancy – bay leaves
Dendromancy – oak and mistletoe
Elaeomancy – water gazing
Extispicy –entrails of animals
Geomancy – earth movement
Gyromancy – whirling persons
Hepatoscopy – liver of animals
Hippomancy – horses
Hydromancy – water
Lampadomancy – flicking torches
Lecanomancy – oil on water

Libanomancy – incense smoke
Lithomancy – polished stones
Lychnomancy – oil lamp flame
Margaritomancy – pearls
Metoscopy – forehead
Molybdomancy – the metal lead
Myomancy – mice squeaks/damage
Nephelomancy – clouds
Numerology – numbers
Oinomancy – goblet & red wine
Ololygmancy – howling of dogs
Oneiromancy – dreams
Onychomancy – nails polished
Oomantia – egg whites
Ornithomancy – birds
Pegomancy – water in fountain
Pessomancy – pebbles
Plastromancy – turtle shells
Phyllorhodomancy – rose leaves
Physiognomy – body/face
Pyromancy – fire
Rhabdomancy – magic wands
Rhapsodomancy – book of poetry
Scyphomancy – cups or vases
Sideromancy – burning straws
Spodomancy – ashes
Stolisomancy – act of dressing
Sycomancy – fig leaves
Tasseography – tea leaves
Tephramancy – wind or breath
Tiromancy – cheese
Xylomancy - wood

NOTES TO INTRODUCTION

1. *Encyclopedia of Religion,* 230.
2. J.H. Manas, *Divination Ancient and Modern* (New York: Pythagorean Society, 1947), 261.
3. Fiery, A.., *The Book of Divination.* (San Francisco: Chronicle Books, 1999), 11.
4. Forman, H. J., *The Story of Prophecy.*(New York: Tudor Publishing Co., 1940), 11.
5. T. W. Overholt, *Channels of Prophecy* (Minneapolis: Fortress Press, 1989), 8.
6. H.J. Forman, *Story of Prophecy,* 18.
7. Ibid., 7.
8. Ibid., Foreword, vii.
9. D. Sutphen, *Past Lives, Future Loves,* (New York: Pocket Books, 1978), 15.
10. J.H. Manas, *Divination, Ancient and Modern,* 3.
11. Wikipedia, 10/11/11.
12. J.H. Manas, *Divination, Ancient and Modern,* 261.
13. H. Reed, *Edgar Cayce on Channeling Your Higher Self,* (New York: Warner Books, 1989), 6.
14. H. Carrington, *Story of Psychic Science,* (New York: Ives Washburn, 1931), 29.
15. H. J. Forman, *Story of Prophecy,* 16.
16. Ibid., 8.
17. Ibid., 9.
18. Ibid., 10.
19. R.R. Springer, *Intra Muros,* (n.p. 1898), 47.
20. Foundation for Inner Peace, *A Course in Mireacles,* (Mill Valley, CA: 1992), 20: II: 8: 1.
21. G. Auzou, *Formation of the Bible,* (London: B. Herder Book Co., 1963), 6.
22. Ibid., 9.
23. B. Worcester, *Swedenborg: Harbinger of the New Age, of the Christian Church* (Philadelphia: J.B. Lippincott Company, 1912), 166.

NOTES

Notes to Chapter 1

1. Editors of Time-Life Books, *Visions and Prophecies*. (Alexandria, VA: Time-Life Books, 1988), 32.
2. *Webster's Collegiate Dictionary.* (Springfield, MA: Merriam-Webster, Inc., 2003).
3. V. Ferm, An *Encyclopedia of Religion* (New York: The Philosophical Library, 1945), 710.
4. J. H. Manas, *Divination Ancient and Modern* (New York: Pythagorean Society, 1947), 17.
5. Ibid., 19-20.
6. Ibid., 20-21.
7. Ibid., 24.
8. Ibid., 25.
9. Ibid., 27-28.
10. Ibid., 50.
11. H. J. Forman, *The Story of Prophecy* (New York: Tudor Publishing Co., 1940), 41.
12. Eds. of Time-Life Books, *Visions and Prophecies*, 33.
13. *Webster's Collegiate Dictionary.*
14. *Encyclopedia of Religion.*
15. Ibid., 615.
16. H. Carrington, *The Story of Psychic Science* (New York: Ives Washburn, 1931), 29.
17. *New College Encyclopedia* (New York: Galahad Books, 1978), 259.
18. C. S. Littleton, ed., *Mythology, The Illustrated Anthology of World Myth and Storytelling* (London: Duncan Baird Publishers, 2002), 185.
19. Forman, *Story of Prophecy*, 21.
20. Carrington, *Story of Psychic Science*, 30.
21. Ibid., 31.

Notes to Chapter 2

1. *Shorter Oxford English Dictionary* (London: Oxford University Press, 1950).
2. G. Auzou, *Formation of the Bible* (London: B. Herder Book Co., 1963), 6.
3. M. Severy, ed., *Great Religions of the World* (Washington, DC: National Geographic Society, 1978), 123.
4. *New College Encyclopedia*, 317-318.
5. *Encyclopedia of Religion*, 615.
6. Auzou, *Formation of the Bible*, 20.
7. Manas, *Divination*, 50.

8. Ibid., 51.
9. Ibid., 21.
10. Ibid.
11. Ibid., 55.
12. *Shorter Oxford Dictionary,* 567.
13. Littleton, *Mythology,* 166.
14. J. Wood, *The Celtic Book of Living and Dying* (San Francisco: Chronicle Books, 2000), 85.
15. Littleton, *Mythology,* 253.
16. Eds. of Time-Life Books, *Visions and Prophecies.* 33.
17. Ibid.

Notes to Chapter 3

1. Forman, *Story of Prophecy,* 74.
2. Manas, *Divination,* 1.
3. H. L. Cayce, *Edgar Cayce on Reincarnation* (New York: Paperback Library, 1967), 146-147.
4. *Encyclopedia of Religion,* 614.
5. Ibid.
6. Manas, *Divination,* 247.
7. A. Fiery, *The Book of Divination.* (San Francisco: Chronicle Books, 1999), 62.
8. C. J. Harrell, *The Bible: Its Origin and Growth.* (Nashville, TN: Cokesbury Press, 1926), 134.
9. Manas, *Divination,* 243.
10. Ibid., 251.
11. *Encyclopedia of Religion,* 615.
12. Manas, *Divination,* 244.
13. *Metaphysical Bible Dictionary.* (Unity Village, MO: Unity School of Christianity, 1931), Preface.
14. Wikipedia, Nov. 2011.
15. *Encyclopedia of Religion,* 615.
16. Manas, *Divination,* 258.
17. *Webster's Collegiate Dictionary,* 58.
18. *Encyclopedia of Religion,* 31.
19. *Lost Books of the Bible and The Forgotten Books of Eded,* (New York: World Publishing Co., 1971), 18.
20. Ibid., 17.
21. Ibid., 40.
22. Ibid., 42.
23. Ibid., 46-47.
24. Auzou, *Formation of the Bible,* 290-291.

Notes to Chapter 4

1. Wikipedia 10/11/10.
2. Manas, *Divination*, 108.
3. Fiery, *Book of Divination*, 84.
4. Manas, *Divination*, 109.
5. Levi, *Aquarian Gospel of Jesus the Christ*, X: 45: 9-20.
6. Overholt, *Channels of Prophecy*, 161.
7. Ibid., 165.
8. Wikipedia, 1/11/10.
9. *Wall Chart of World History*. (London: Studio Editions Ltd., 1988).
10. Forman, *Story of Prophecy*, 130.
11. Ibid., 141.
12. Fiery, *Book of Divination*, 60.
13. Eds. of Time-Life Books, *Mysteries of the Unknown: Psychic Powers*, 18.
14. Forman, *Story of Prophecy*, 34.
15. *Encyclopedia of Religion*, 827.
16. Littleton, *Mythology*, 580.
17. Ibid., 603-604.
18. Ibid., 604.
19. Ibid.
20. Forman, *Story of Prophecy*, 194.

Notes to Chapter 5

1. Forman, *Story of Prophecy*, 156.
2. Ibid., 4-5.
3. Ibid., 159.
4. S. Schneidman and P. Daniels, eds., *Mysteries of the Unknown: Visions and Prophecies*, 45.
5. Ibid.
6. Ibid., 36.
7. Forman, *Story of Prophecy*, 11.
8. Ibid., 13.
9. Littleton, *Mythology*, 632.
10. Forman, *Story of Prophecy*, 5.
11. Ibid.
12. *Encyclopedia of Religion*, 827.
13. Forman, *Story of Prophecy*, 220.
14. B. Worcester, *Swedenborg: Harbinger of the New Age of the Christian Church.* (Philadelphia: J.B. Lippincott Company, 1912), 244.
15. E. Swedenborg, *Divine Providence.* (West Chester, PA: Swedenborg Foundation, 2003), translator's Preface, 1.
16. E. Swedenborg, *Heavenly Secrets.* (West Chester, PA: Swedenborg Foundation, 1998), 2-3.

17. E. Swedenborg, *Heaven and Hell*, (West Chester, PA: Swedenborg Foundation, 2000), 536.
18. Worcester, *Swedenborg: Harbinger of the New Age*, 148-149.
19. Ibid., 172.
20. Ibid., 242.
21. M. A. Larson, *New Thought or A Modern Religious Approach*. (New York: Philosophical Library, 1985), 34-35.
22. Carrington, *Story of Psychic Science*, 39.
23. *Shorter Oxford English Dictionary*, 944.
24. Prince, W. F., *Noted Witnesses for Psychic Occurrences*. (New Hyde Park, NY: University Books, 1963), 136.
25. Forman, *Story of Prophecy*, 233.
26. M.A. Warner and D. Beilenson, eds. *Women of Faith and Spirit*. (White Plains, NY: Peter Pauper Press, Inc., 1987), 18

Notes to Chapter 6
1. *Webster's Collegiate Dictionay.*
2. Warner and Beilenson, *Women of Faith and Spirit*, 35.
3. R. Stemman, *Spirits and Spirit World*. (London: Robert B. Clark, 1975), 6.
4. Forman, *Story of Prophecy*, 52.
5. Prince, *Noted Witnesses*, 121-122.
6. Prince, *Noted Witnesses*, 126.
7. Carrington, *Story of Psychic Science*, 50.
8. Prince, *Noted Witnesses*, 257.
9. Overholt, *Channels of Prophecy*, 28.
10. Springer, *Intramuros*, 47.
11. Forman, *Story of Prophecy*, 302.
12. Ibid., 305.
13. Ibid., 306.

Notes to Chapter 7
1. Three Initiates, *The Kybalion*. (Clayton, GA: Tri-State Press, 1988), 178-179.
2. Forman, *Story of Prophecy*, 6.
3. B. T. Spaulding, *Life and Teaching of the Masters of the Far East, Vol.1*. (Marina del Rey, CA: De Vorss and Company, 1964), 53-54.
4. Ibid., 80-81.
5. Eds. of Time-Life Books. *Mysteries of the Unknown: Phantom Encounters*. (Alexandria, VA: Time-Life Books, 1988), 67.
6. J. T. Ferrier, J. T., *The Logia or Sayings of the Master*. (London: The Order of the Cross, 1991), 387.

7. Eds. of Time-Life Books, *Mysteries of the Unknown: Visions and Prophecies.* (Alexandria, VA: Time-Life Books, 1988), 44.

8. A. Bancroft, *Twentieth Century Mystics and Sages* (Chicago: Henry Regnery Company, 1976), 256.

9. Ibid., 264.

10. J. Furst, ed., *Edgar Cayce's Story of Attitudes and Emotions.*(New York: Berkley Medallion Books, 1972), 13.

11. H. H. Bro, *Edgar Cayce on Dreams.* (New York: Warner Books, 1968), Intro, 7.

12. E. Cayce, *My Life as a Seer.* (New York: St. Martins' Press, 1999), 14-15.

13. Ibid., 268-269.

14. J. Furst, ed., *Edgar Cayce's Story of Jesus.* (New York: Berkley Books, 1976), Intro, 9-10.

15. D. Agee and H.L. Cayce, eds., *Edgar Cayce on ESP.* (New York: Paperback Library, 1969), 11.

16. Ibid.

17. Ibid., 10.

18. R. A. Karp, *Edgar Cayce Encyclopedia of Healing.* (New York: Warner Books, 1986), 3.

19. G. Cerminara, *Many Mansions.* (New York: New American Library, 1950), 73.

20. E. Cayce, *My Life as a Seer,* 11.

21. Saint Germain, *The "I AM" Discourses.* ((Schaumburg, IL: St. Germain Press, Inf., 1988), Foreword, xiii.

22. C. Wilson, *Mysterious Powers.* (n.p.: The Danbury Press, 1975), 124.

23. Ellison, J., ed., *The Life Beyond Death.* (New York: Berkley Publishing Corp., 1972), back cover.

24. A. Borgia, *Life in the World Unseen.* (London: Odhams Press Limited, 1958), 49.

25. Forman, *Story of Prophecy* , 257.

26. Ibid., 264.

27. Borgia, *Life in the World Unseen,* Preface.

28. Ibid.

29. Ibid. 191.

30. K. McConnell, *Don't Call Them Ghosts.* (Woodbury, MN: Llewellyn Publications, 2007), back cover.

31. Ibid., 243

32. J. Boss, *In Silence They Return.* (St. Paul, MN: Llewellyn Publications, 1972), 93.

33. A. A. Worrall and O. Worall, *The Gift of Healing.* (Columbus, O: Ariel Press, 1985), 114.

34. Eds. of Time-Life Books, *Mysteries of the Unknown: Psychic Powers,* 78-79.

35. H. Reed, *Edgar Cayce on Channeling Your Higher Self* (New York: Warner Books, 1989), 6.

36. A. Meurois-Givaudan and D. Meurois-Givaudan, *The Way of the Essenes.* (Rochester, VT: Destiny Books, 1993), Intro, viii..

Notes to Chapter 8

1. P. Donovan and M. I. Lee-Civalier, *Getting to Know Your Soul.* (New York: iUniverse, Inc., 2004), 59.

2. Levi, *The Aquarian Gospel of Jesus the Christ.* (Marina del Rey, CA: DeVorss & Co., 1980), 39:11-18.

3. Forman, *Story of* Prophecy, 304.

4. Meurois-Givaudan, *The Way of the Essenes, Intro, ix.*

5. Ibid., 260.

6. The Christ, *New Teachings for an Awakening Humanity.* (Santa Clara, CA: Spiritual Education Endeavors, 1994), Foreword, i-ii.

7. G. C. Porter and G. K. Lippmann, *Conversations with JC.* (Piermont, NY: High View Publishing, 1985), Intro, 3.

Notes to Chapter 9

1. Wikipedia, 1/30/12, Lisa Ling Interview.

2. Ibid.

3. M. Dolan, *I Know Why We're Here.* (New York: Harmony Books, 2003), book jacket.

4. H. Sherman, *The Dead are Alive.* (New York: Fawcett Gold Medal, 1981),17.

5. R. Moody, *Reunions.* (New York: Random House, 1993), Intro, x.

6. R. Stemman, *Spirits and Spirit Worlds.* (n. p.: Robert B. Clark, publ., 1975), 22.

7. Ibid.

8. Ibid., 21.

9. Ibid.

10. Malz. B., *My Glimpse of Eternity.* (Carmel, N. Y.: Guideposts, 1978), Prologue, 15.

11. Ibid., 89.

12. G.G. Ritchie, *Return from Tomorrow.* (Carmel, N.Y.: Guideposts, 1978), 15-16.

13. Borgia, *Life in the World Unseen,* 12.

14. R.Montgomery, *A World Beyond.* (New York:: Fawcett Crest, 1971), 10.

15. H. Sherman, *The Dead are Alive,* 38.

16. *A Course in Miracles.* (Mill Valley, CA: Foundation for Inner Peace, 1992), 2:I:3:6-8.

17. I. Cook, ed., *The Return of Arthur Conan Doyle.* (Liss, England: White Eagle Publishing Trust, 1975), Preface, vii.

18. S. E. White, *The Unobstructed Universe.* (New York: E.P. Dutton & Co., Inc., 1940), 33.

19. J. A. Pike, *The Other Side.* (Garden City, NY: Doubleday &Co., Inc., 1968), 384.

20. B. and S. H. Steiger, *Children of the Light.* (New York: Penguin Books, 1995), 68.

21. Ibid., 122.

22. Ibid., 131-132.

23. N. D. Walsch, *Conversations with God.* (New York: G. P. Putnam's Sons, 1996), 1-2.

24. R. Stemman, *Spirits and Spirit Worlds.*, 90.

25. B. O. Bristow, *The Universal Consciousness.* (Ocala, FL: privately printed, 2009), Preface.

26. Ibid., 55-56.

27. Ibid., 24.

28. Wikipedia, 1/30/12.

29. E. S. and F. L. Holmes, *The Voice Celestial.* (New York: Dodd, Mead and Co. n.d), 78.

30. J. H. Manas, *Divination Ancient and Modern.* (New York: Pythagorean Society, 1947), 263.

Notes to Chapter 10

1. Cayce, *My Life as a Seer,* 14.

2. A. Myers, *Communicating with Animals.* (Chicago: Contemporary Books, 1997), Preface, ix.

3. H. Reed, *Edgar Cayce on Channeling Your Higher Self.* (New York: Warner Books, 1989), 268.

4. J. Wylder, *Psychic Pets.* (New York: Harper and Row, 1978), Intro, xii.

5. B. Schul, *The Psychic Power of Animals.* (Greenwich, CT: Fawcett Publications, Inc., 1977), 11-13.

6. A. Myers, *Communicating with Animals.* (Chicago: Contemporary Books, 1997), 200.

7. H. Holzer, *The Psychic World of Plants.* (New York: Pyramid Books, 1975), Intro, 18.

8. The Findhorn Community, *The Findhorn Garden.* (New York: Harper and Row, 1975), Foreword, 11.

9. Ibid., 152.

10. Ibid., 6.

11. Ibid., 41-42.

12. Ibid., 57.

13. Ibid., 58.

14. Ibid., 125.

15. Ibid., 129.

16. *Findhorn*, 172.
17. Ibid., 10.
18. Ibid., 73.
19. Ibid., 162.
20. M. S. Wright, *Behaving as if the God in all Life Mattered.* (Jeffersonton, GA: Perelandra Ltd., 1987), 86.
21. Ibid., Intro, 13.
22. H. Holzer, *The Psychic World of Plants*, 116.
23. M. D'Andrea, *Psychic Vibrations of Crystals, Gems & Stones.* (New Brunswick, NJ: Inner Light Publications, 1988), Intro, 4.
24. Wright, *Behaving as if the God in all Life Mattered*, 160-161.
25. H. B. Puryear, *The Edgar Cayce Primer.* (New York: Bantam Books, 1986), 6.
26. Reed, *Edgar Cayce on Channeling Your Higher Self*, 272.
27. *A Course in Miracles*, Workbook Part II, Intro, 5:1-7.

Notes to Chapter 11

1. Forman, *The Story of Prophecy*, 264.
2. Worcester, *Swedenborg: Harbinger of the New Age*, 244.
3. Ibid., 172.
4. Ibid., 242.
5. Bancroft, *Twentieth Century Mystics and Sages*, 256.
6. Ibid., 264.
7. Cayce, *My Life as a Seer*, 14-15.
8. Ellison, *The Life Beyond Death*, back cover.
9. Moody, *Reunions*, Intro, x.
10. Stemman, *Spirits and Spirit Worlds*, 22.
11. Meurois-Givaudan, *The Way of the Essenes*, 260.
12. Levi, *Aquarian Gospel of Jesus the Christ*, 43:11.
13. Ibid., 68:16-20
14. Holmes, *The Voice Celestial*, 313.
15. Meurois-Givaudan, *The Way of the Essenes*, 260.
16. Forman, *The Story of Prophecy*, 536.
17. Ibid., 34.
18. *Encyclopedia of Religion*, 827.
19. Ibid., 464
20. Prince, *Note Witnesses for Psychic Occurrences*, 257.
21. Pike, *The Other Side*, 384.
22. St. Germain, *The "I AM" Discourses*, Foreword, xiii.
23. Boss, *In Silence They Return*, 93.
24. Dolan, M., *I Know Why We're Here.* (New York: Harmony Books, 2003), book jacket.
25. The Christ, *New Teachings*, 1.

26. Bristow, *Universal Consciousness*, Preface.
27. Ibid., 55-56.
28. Ibid., 24.
29. The Christ, *New Teachings*, 260.
30. Montgomery, *A World Beyond*, 10.
31. Walsch, *Conversations with God*, 1-2.
32. Stemman, *Spirits and Spirit Worlds*, 90.
33. *Shorter Oxford English Dictionary*, 944.
34. Levi, *Aquarian Gospel of Jesus the Christ*, 39:11-18.
35. Agee, *Edgar Cayce on ESP*, 65.
36. Stemman, *Spirits and Spirit Worlds*, 76.
37. Ibid., 79.
38. Ibid., 78.
39. Worcester, *Swedenborg: Harbinger of the New Age*, 148-149.
40. Prince, *Noted Witnesses*, 121-122.
41. Ibid., 125-126.
42. Springer, *Intramuros*, 47.
43. Stemman, *Spirits and Spirit Worlds*, 21.
44. Ibid.
45. Ferrier, *The Logia*, 387.
46. Bro, *Edgar Cayce on Dreams*, 7.
47. St. Germain, *The Magic Presence*, Tribute, vi.
48. Stemman, *Spirits and Spirit Worlds*, 22.
49. Swedenborg, *Divine Providence*, 1.
50. Cayce, *My Life as a Seer*, 14-15.
51. Manas, *Divination*, 21.
52. Ibid., 50.
53. Carrngton, *Story of Psychic Science*, 30.
54. Fiery, *The Book of Divination*, 84.
55. Forman, *Story of Prophecy*, 141.
56. Ibid., 4-5.
57. Worcester, *Swedenborg: Harbinger of the New Age*, 242.
58. Forman, *Story of Prophecy*, 306.

Notes to Chapter 12

1. B. T. Spaulding, *Life and Teaching of the Masters of the Far East Vol.1*. (Marina del Rey, CA: DeVorss and Company, 1964), 80-81.
2. T. E. Witherspoon, *Myrtle Fillmore: Mother of Unity*. (Unity Village, MO: Unity Books, 1984), 38-40.
3. *Quest for the Unknown: New Age Healing*. Pleasantville, NY: Readers Digest Assoc., 1992), 58. From *I Believe in Miracles* by Kuhlman.
4. Ibid., 64.

5. A. M. Josephy, *500 Nations*. (New York: Gramercy Books, 2002), 305-306.
6. Stemman, *Spirits and Spirit Worlds*, 22.
7. Eds. Time-Life Books, *Psychic Powers*, 23.
8. Porter and Lippmann, *Conversations with JC*, 3.
9. McConnell, *Don't Call Them Ghosts*, 136-137.
10. K Malarkey and A. Malarkey, *The Boy Who Came Back From Heaven*. (Carol Stream, IL: Tyndale House Publishers, Inc., 2011), 14.
11. Ibid., 166.
12. E. Swedenborg, *Heavenly Secrets*. (West Chester, PA: Swedenborg Foundation, 1998), 2-3.
13. Spaulding, *Life and Teachings of the Masters Vol. 1*, 53-54.
14. Steiger, *Children of the Light*, 122.
15. Lewis and Oliver, *Angels A to Z*. (Canton, MI: Visible Ink Press, 2002), Foreword, xi.
16. Stemman, *Spirits and Spirit Worlds*, 57.
17. Ibid., 82.
18. Malarkey, *Boy Who Came Back*, 86.
19. Ibid., 86-87.
20. Stemman, *Spirits and Spirit Worlds*, 38.
21. Ibid., 40.
22. Sherman, *The Dead are Alive*, 38.
23. *Metaphysical Bible Dictionary*.

Glossary

Akashic Records –
" . . .The word *akasha* is a Sanskrit term referring to one of the constituents of the natural world, the other ones being earth, water, fire and air. According to ancient tradition, it is an infinitely subtle substance, a form of energy in which the universe bathes, and which is capable of storing the visual and auditive memory of all life." P.viii Inro way of Essenes

Apocrypha
Books included in the Septuagint and Vulgate but excluded from t he Jewish and Protestant canons of the Old Testament. (MW11th)

Apports
A physical phenomena in which animate or inanimate things materialize and thus become visible to the human eye.

Automatic writing
MW 11th ed!!!!!!!!!: writing produced without conscious intention as if of telepathic or spiritualistic origin

Clairaudient
The ability to hear spirit.

Clairsentient
The ability to 'sense' spirit and derive a message from it.

Clairvoyant
The ability to see spirit.

Divination
1. From Merriam-Webster, 11th ed.:1.The art or practice that seeks to foresee or foretell future events or discover hidden knowledge usu. by the interpretation of omens by the aid of supernatural powers. 2. unusual insight. Intuitive perception.

2. The New College Encyclopedia: specifies events of the past and present, also: "the act of obtaining knowledge of things past, present, or future, by supernatural revelation."

Familiar or familiar spirit
As a noun, this is synonymous with a psychic or medium.

Inspirational speaking
Speaking words of divine influence. Speaking without physical notes, receiving and speaking words that flow from spirit through the speaker, while fully awake. To present words of guidance from an unseen entity.

Materialization
Manifestation in physical form of a spirit entity. Jesus materialized after the resurrection.

Medium
A psychic who sees beyond the astral plane and into the akashic records

Mental phenomena
Supernatural events that are not seen but known.

Metaphysical
Of or relating to he transcendent or to a reality beyond what is perceptible to the senses. Supernatural.

Oracle
". . . in classic antiquity, the response of a god to a question asked by a worshipper; also the place where the response was given. Of the many ancient oracular shrines, the Greek oracles, notably those of Zeus at Olympia and Apollo at Delphi, attained the greatest importance. The general reputation of the oracle for honesty and wisdom made it the highest authority in Greek morals and religion." The New College Encyclopedia (1978, New York Galahad Books), p.651

Paranormal
Not scientifically explainable.

163

Physical phenomena
Supernatural events that materialize in physical form and are visible apparent to the human eye. The burning bush in the Bible (Ex. 3:2) is an example.

Psychic
A person who can read from the energy and thoughts of another.

Revelation
An act of relating or communicating divine truth. Something that is revealed by God to humans.

Scrying
Reading from the spirit world by gazing at a flat, brilliant surface.

Séance
A group of individuals who set quietly in a circle and seek to receive messages psychically from the spirit world.

Seer
Interpreter of signs provided by the gods.

Speaking in tongues
The act of speaking aloud in an unknown tongue; probably while in trance. To understand the words an interpreter is required.

Spirit levitation
The act of raising a body off the floor by supernatural means

Spiritual gifts
The gifts of the spirit are described in I Cor. 12:1-10:
Wisdom, knowledge, faith, healing, miracles, prophecy, discerning of spirits, diverse tongues, interpreting tongues.

Supernatural
Of or relating to an order of existence beyond the visible observable universe; esp: of or relating to God or a god, demigod, spirit, or devil.

Trance

Full trance: The person giving the message is completely unaware of what is being said through him/her by a spirit entity.

Partial trance: The person giving the message is aware of what s/he is saying while giving an inspired message from spirit.

Bibliography

BOOKS

A Course in Miracles. Mill Valley, CA: Foundation for Inner Peace, 1992.

Agee, D. and Cayce, H. L., ed., *Edgar Cayce on ESP.* New York: Paperback Library, 1969

Auzou, G., *The Formation of the Bible.* London: B. Herder Book Co., 1963. Trans. By Josefa Thornton. First published, *LaTradition biblique*, Paris: Editions de l'Orante, 1957.

Bancroft, A.., *Twentieth Century Mystics and Sages.* Chicago: Henry Regnery Company, 1976.

Barnard, J., ed., *Keats: The Complete Poems, Third edition.* London: Penguin Books, 1988.

Borgia, A., *Life in the World Unseen.* London: Odhams Press Limited, 1958.

Boss, J., *In Silence They Return.* St. Paul, MN: Llewellyn Publications, 1972.

Bristow, B.O., *The Universal Consciousness.* Ocala, FL: privately printed, 2009.

Bro, H.H., *Edgar Cayce on Dreams.* New York: Warner Books, 1968.

Carrington, H., *The Story of Psychic Science.* New York: Ives Washburn, 1931.

Cayce, E., *My Life as a Seer.* New York: St. Martins' Press, 1999. Originally published as *The Lost Memoirs of Edgar Cayce*, Virginia Beach, VA, A.R.E. Press, 1997.

Cayce, H.L., *Edgar Cayce on Reincarnation.* New York: Paperback Library, 1967.
_____*Venture Inward.* New Yok:Paperback Library, 1968.

Cerminara, G. *Many Mansions.* New York: New American Library, 1950.

The Christ, *New Teachings for an Awakening Humanity.* Santa Clara, CA: Spiritual Education Endeavors, 1994 (1986).

Cook, I., ed., *The Return of Arthur Conan Doyle..* Liss, England: White Eagle Publishing Trust, 1975.

Cunningham, S., *Divination for Beginners*. St. Paul, MN: Llewellyn Publications, 2003.

D'Andrea, M., *Psychic Vibrations of Crystals, Gems & Stones*. New Brunswick, NJ: Inner Light Publications, 1988.

Del Mar, E., *Spiritual and Material Attraction*. Denver: Smith-Brooks Printing Co., 1901.

Dolan, M., *I Know Why We're Here*. New York: Harmony Books, 2003.

Donovan, P. and Lee-Civalier, M. I., *Getting to Know Your Soul*. New York: iUniverse, Inc., 2004.

Editors of Time-Life Books, *Mysteries of the Unknown: Psychic Powers*. Alexandria, VA: Time-Life Books, 1987.

_____*Mysteries of the Unknown: Visions and Prophecies*. Alexandria, VA: Time-Life Books, 1988.

_____*Mysteries of the Unknown: Phantom Encounters*. Alexandria, VA: Time-Life Books, 1988.

Ellison, J., ed., *The Life Beyond Death*. New York: Berkley Publishing Corp., 1972.

Emoto, M., *Messages from Water*. n.d.: Hado Publishing, 1999.

Ferm, V., *An Encyclopedia of Religion*. New York: The Philosophical Library, 1945.

Ferrier, J. T., *The Logia or Sayings of the Master*. London: The Order of the Cross, 1991 (1916).

Fiery, A.., *The Book of Divination*. San Francisco: Chronicle Books, 1999.

The Findhorn Community, *The Findhorn Garden*. New York: Harper and Row, 1975.

Forman, H. J., *The Story of Prophecy*. New York: Tudor Publishing Co., 1940.

Furst, J. ed., *Edgar Cayce's Story of Attitudes and Emotions*. New York: Berkley Medallion Books, 1972.

167

_____ *Edgar Cayce's Story of Jesus*. New York: Berkley Books, 1976.

Greber, J., trans. from the German., *Communication with The Spirit World of God*. Teaneck, NJ: Johannes Greber Memorial Foundation, 1974 (1932) .

Harrell, C. J., *The Bible: Its Origin and Growth*. Nashville, TN: Cokesbury Press, 1926.

Harris, B., *Journey into the Spirit World*. The Spiritualist Assoc. of Great Britain, nd, nc.

Holmes, E. S. and Holmes, F. L., *The Voice Celestial.*. New York: Dodd, Mead and Co. n.d.

Holy Bible, AV.

Holzer, H., *The Psychic World of Plants.*. New York: Pyramid Books, 1975.

Josephy, A. M., *500 Nations*. New York: Gramercy Books, 2002.

Kagan N. and Daniels, Pat, ed., *Mysteries of the Unknown: Psychic Powers*. Alexandria, VA: Time-Life Books, Inc., 1987.

Karp, R. A., *Edgar Cayce Encyclopedia of Healing*. New York: Warner Books, 1986.

Larson, M.A., *New Thought or A Modern Religious Approach*. New York: Philosophical Library, 1985.

Levi, *The Aquarian Gospel of Jesus the Christ*. Marina del Rey, CA: DeVorss & Co., 1980 (1907).

Lewis, J. R. and Oliver, E. D., *Angels A to Z*. Canton, MI: Visible Ink Press, 2002.

Littleton, C.S., gen. ed., *Mythology, The Illustrated Anthology of World Myth and Storytelling*. London: Duncan Baird Publishers, 2002.

Lost Books of the Bible and The Forgotten Books of Eden.. New York: The World Publishing Company, 1971 (Alpha House © 1926 ; Forgotten Books of Eden Alpha House © 1927).

Malarkey, K. and Malarkey, A. , *The Boy Who Came Back From Heaven*. Carol Stream, IL: Tyndale House Publishers, Inc., 2011.

Malz. B., *My Glimpse of Eternity*. Carmel, N. Y.: Guideposts, 1978.

Manas, J. H., *Divination Ancient and Modern*. New York: Pythagorean Society, 1947.

McConnell, K., *Don't Call Them Ghosts*. Woodbury, MN: Llewellyn Publications, 2007.

Merriam-Webster's Collegiate Dictionary, Eleventh Edition. Springfield, MA: Merriam Webster, Inc., 2005.

Metaphysical Bible Dictionary. Unity Village, MO: Unity School of Christianity, 1931.

Meurois-Givaudan, A. and Meurois-Givaudan, D., *The Way of the Essenes*. Rochester, VT: Destiny Books, 1993. First published in French under the title *De Memoire d'Essenien, Pautre Visage de Jesus* by Arista Editions, Plazac, 1989.

Montgomery, R. *A World Beyond*. New York:: Fawcett Crest, 1971.

Moody, R., A.*Life After Life*. New York: Bantam Books, 1988.

_____*Reunions*. New York: Random House, 1993.

Myers, A., *Communicating with Animals*. Chicago: Contemporary Books, 1997.

The New College Encyclopedia. New York: Galahad Books, 1968.

Overholt, T. W., *Channels of Prophecy*. Minneapolis: Fortress Press, 1989.

Pike, J. A., *The Other Side.*. Garden City, NY: Doubleday &Co., Inc., 1968.

Porter, G. C. and Lippmann, G. K., *Conversations with JC*. Piermont, NY: High View Publishing, 1985.

Prince, W. F., *Noted Witnesses for Psychic Occurrences*. New Hyde Park, NY: University Books, 1963. Copyright 1928 by Boston Society for Psychic Research.

Puryear, H. B., *The Edgar Cayce Primer*. New York: Bantam Books, 1986.

Quest for the Unkown: New Age Healing. Pleasantville, NY: Readers Digest Assoc., 1992.

Reed, H.., *Edgar Cayce on Channeling Your Higher Self*. New York: Warner Books, 1989.

Ritchie, G.G., *Return from Tomorrow.*. Carmel, N.Y.: Guideposts, 1978.

Saint Germain, *The Magic Presence*. Schaumburg, IL: St. Germain Press, Inc., 1982 (1935).

_____*The "I AM" Discourses*. Schaumburg, IL: St. Germain Press, Inc., 1988 (1935).

Schneidman, S. and Daniels,Pat, ed., *Mysteries of the Unknown: Phantom Encounters*. Alexandria, VA: Time-Life Books, Inc., 1988.

_____*Mysteries of the Unknown: Visions and Prophecies*. Alexandria, VA: Time-Life Books, Inc., 1988.

Schul, B., *The Psychic Power of Animals*. Greenwich, CT: Fawcett Publications, Inc., 1977.

Severy, M. ed., *Great Religions of the World*. Washington, D.C.: National Geographic Society, 1978.

Sherman, H., *The Dead are Alive*. New York: Fawcett Gold Medal, 1981.

Shorter Oxford English Dictionary. Glasgow: Oxford University Press, 1950.

Smith, A. R., ed., *My Life as a Seer*. New York: St. Martin's Press, 1997(1971).

Spaulding, B. T., *Life and Teaching of the Masters of the Far East, Vol.1,*. Marina del Rey, CA: DeVorss and Company, 1964 (1924).

Springer, R. R., *Into the Light*. Originally published as *Intra Muros*, n.p., 1898. Shakopee, MN: Macalester Park Publishing, 1994.

Steiger, B. and Steiger, S.H., *Children of the Light*. New York: Penguin Books, 1995.

Stemman, R., *Spirits and Spirit Worlds*. London: Aldus Books, Ltd., 1975.

Stearn, J., *Edgar Cayce – The Sleeping Prophet*. New York: Doubleday & Company, 1967.

Sutphen, D., *Past lives, Future Loves*. New York: Pocket Books, 1978.

Swedenborg, E., *Heavenly Secrets*. Clowes, J., trans., West Chester, PA: Swedenborg Foundation, 1998. First publ. in Latin, 1749.

_____*Heaven and Hell*. Dole, G. F., trans., West Chester, PA: Swedenborg Foundation, 2000.

_____*Divine Providence*. Dole, G. F., trans., West Chester, PA: Swedenborg Foundation, 2003.

The Christ, *New Teachings for an Awakening Humanity*. Santa Clara, CA: Spiritual Education Endeavors, 1994.

Three Initiates, *The Kybalion*. Clayton, GA: Tri-State Press, 1988. Originally published by Yogi Publication Society, 1908.

Von Daniken, E., *Chariots of the Gods?* M. Horn, trans. New York: G. P. Putnam & Sons, 1968.

Versluis, A., *Sacred Earth*. Rochester, VT: Inner Traditions International, 1992.

Wall Chart of World History. London: Studio Editions. Ltd., 1988. Facsimile Edition by Barnes and Noble Publishing, Inc., 1995.

Walsch, N. D., *Conversations with God*. New York: G.P.Putnam's Sons, 1996.

Warner, M.A. and Beilenson, D., eds. *Women of Faith and Spirit*. White Plains, NY: Peter Pauper Press, Inc., 1987.

Whiston, W., trans., *Josephus*. Grand Rapids, MI: Kregel Publications, 1967.

White, S. E., *The Unobstructed Universe*. New York: E.P. Dutton & Co., Inc., 1940.

Wigginton, E., ed., *The Foxfire Book*. Garden City: Anchor Books., 1972.

Wilson, C., *Mysterious Powers*. n.p.: The Danbury Press, 1975. First published by Aldus Ltd, London, 1975.

Witherspoon, T.E., *Myrtle Fillmore, Mother of Unity*. Unity Village, MO: Unity Books, 1984.

Wood, J., *The Celtic Book of Living and Dying*. San Francisco: Chronicle Books, 2000.

Worcester, B., *Swedenborg: Harbinger of the New Age of the Christian Church*. Philadelphia: J.B. Lippincott Company, 1912.

Worrall, A. A. and Worall, O., *The Gift of Healing*. Columbus, O: Ariel Press, 1985(1965).

Wright, M. S., *Behaving as if the God in all Life Mattered*. Jeffersonton, GA: Perelandra Ltd., 1987.

Wylder, J., *Psychic Pets*. New York: Harper and Row, 1978.

OTHER
Archangel Gabriel teachings
Booklets: *Spiritual Evolution of Humankind*, March 5, 1999.
DISCOGRAPHY:
     Internal Awareness. 5/18/96
     Connecting to Your Source. 11/15/97
     Angels, Aliens & Earthlings. 7/27/91

Note: All the teachings of Archangel Gabriel and Master Jesus are available at jackleeciv@nycap.rr.com or see Sacred Garden Fellowship.org

WEBSITES
abebooks.com
Guardian.co.uk
Sacredgardenfellowship.org
Wikipedia.org